Woodrow
Wilson

Woodrow

Wilson

A BRIEF BIOGRAPHY

by Arthur S. Link

THE WORLD PUBLISHING COMPANY

Cleveland and New York

Published by The World Publishing Company
2231 West 110th Street, Cleveland 2, Ohio
Published simultaneously in Canada by
Nelson, Foster & Scott Ltd.
Library of Congress Catalog Card Number: 63-8980
Third Printing
3WP1166
Designed by Jack Jaget

For

JOHN WELLS DAVIDSON AND DAVID W. HIRST
friends and colleagues

CONTENTS

PREFACE

I have prepared this little book to serve as an introduction to the life and times of Woodrow Wilson for students and general readers. I should be very much disappointed if readers, particularly young readers, regarded it as anything more than a beginning of their own inquiry. I trust that I have painted a reliable word portrait of Wilson the man, and placed him in the context of events in which he played a significant role. But I have been able in a book of this length to do no more than tell the essence, and I hope readers will want to go on to discover the fuller truth about the man and his times that is revealed in his own writings and speeches and in more detailed biographies and historical monographs.

I think I also owe my readers additional explana-
tion about three things that I have *not* tried to do.
I have avoided, first of all, commenting on certain
recent interpretations that attempt to explain Wilson's allegedly complex personality in Freudian
terms. Wilson, as I view him, was essentially a simple
man, whose life and career were guided as much by
Christian faith as is possible in any human being. But
faith for him did not mean living by rules. It meant
doing the right thing—that is, living obediently—as
best one could in changing circumstances. If this be
true, then an interpretation of Wilson as a simple
moralist, which some other writers have given, also
misses the mark. I have also tried to avoid passing
judgment by saying that what Wilson did on specific
occasions was right or wrong, wise or foolish. I will be
satisfied if I have succeeded in presenting the basic
facts from which readers can form their own con-
clusions. Finally, I have resisted the temptation to
write a concluding assessment of Wilson's significance in modern history. It seems to me that this
ought to come out clearly in an account of his career.

It seemed inappropriate—and literally impossible
—to provide footnote documentation for such a book
as this. I have covered well-trod biographical and historical ground and said virtually nothing that is not
well known to specialists, and readers who want specific documentation will find it in the large literature
on Wilson and his time. Quotations from Wilson's
speeches, statements, and letters have come usually
from *The Public Papers of Woodrow Wilson,* edited

by Ray S. Baker and William E. Dodd, and from
Wilson's letters in the Library of Congress and news-
paper files. Quotations from Wilson's conversations
have been drawn largely from Edith Bolling Wilson,
My Memoir; Cary T. Grayson, *Woodrow Wilson, An
Intimate Memoir;* and, in two instances, from George
F. Sparks (ed.), *A Many-Colored Toga, The Diary of
Henry Fountain Ashurst.* The bibliographical note
at the end of the book includes only basic sources,
biographies, and historical works. Readers who want
to go further might look at the bibliographies in my
Woodrow Wilson and the Progressive Era (Harper
Torchbooks, 1963) and *American Epoch, A History
of the United States Since the 1890's* (Alfred A.
Knopf, Inc., 1963).

I take this opportunity to thank Dr. Arthur M.
Schlesinger, Jr., editor of The American Presidents
Series, for inviting me to write this book and reading
the manuscript helpfully; Dr. Thomas H. Spence, Jr.,
of the Historical Foundation in Montreat, North
Carolina, for his hospitality while I was writing the
first draft of this book; my wife, Mrs. Margaret
Douglas Link, for editorial help in the final stages;
and my colleagues in *The Papers of Woodrow
Wilson,* Dr. John Wells Davidson and Dr. David W.
Hirst, for reading the manuscript critically. The dedi-
cation is a small token of my esteem and affection
for them.

September 22, 1962
Firestone Library Princeton University

                                        ARTHUR S. LINK

Woodrow
Wilson 🌾

Chapter One

TRAINING FOR GREATNESS

"My earliest recollection," Woodrow Wilson said in 1909, "is of standing at my father's gateway in Augusta, Georgia, when I was four years old, and hearing some one pass and say that Mr. Lincoln was elected and there was to be war." Tribal memories are dim at the age of four, but young Thomas Woodrow Wilson soon knew them well enough. There had been Wilsons and Woodrows in Scotland and northern Ireland almost since the beginning of time. They came, went, and intermarried, leaving few written records in their homelands. Many of them also joined the mighty human tide surging to the New World in the eighteenth and early nineteenth centuries in search of economic opportunity and religious and political freedom. One among the multitude was James Wilson, who migrated from northern Ireland to Philadelphia in 1807 and settled in Steubenville, Ohio, after a brief stay in the eastern city. One of his sons, Joseph Ruggles Wilson, entered the Presbyterian ministry and, after marrying Jessie Woodrow, accepted a call to teach at Hampden-Sydney College in Virginia, in 1851. He moved in 1854 to the First Presbyterian Church in nearby Staunton. It was in the handsome brick manse in that town that their first son and second child was born, on December 28, 1856. They named him Thomas Woodrow for his mother's father, a Scottish Presbyterian minister who had settled in Ohio.

Young Tommy Wilson saw enough during boyhood to make him forever loathe war and civil strife. His first memories were of Augusta, where his father served as minister of the First Presbyterian Church from 1857 to 1870—of wounded soldiers in his father's church, of Yankee prisoners in a nearby stockade, of frightening rumors of Sherman and his avenging horde. When the Wilson family moved in 1870 to Columbia, South Carolina, Tommy could see the charred remains of that once beautiful city, burned after Sherman's march, and feel the tensions generated by radical reconstruction in the state. Yet, in spite of the turbulence of public events, his boyhood was remarkably normal. He had the "unspeakable joy," as he once said, of "having been born and bred in a minister's family," one that treasured literature and knew the meaning of moral certitude. His father was a learned theologian, widely read in contemporary affairs, and Stated Clerk of the General Assembly of the Presbyterian Church in the United States (the Southern body) from 1865 until 1898. He superintended the education of his children, and he mixed sternness and sarcasm with affection in demanding intellectual excellence. He was, Woodrow Wilson later said, "one of the most inspiring fathers that a lad was ever blessed with" and "the best instructor, the most inspiring companion . . . that a youngster ever had." He was incomparably the most important influence in Woodrow Wilson's early life.

Next to the home the church was most important in shaping Tommy Wilson during the formative years. He literally grew up in the midst of the Southern Presbyterian Church and imbibed almost unconsciously its traditions and faith in a loving sovereign God Who turns all things to good for those who love Him. Church attendance, prayer, and reading of the Bible were from childhood part of the routine of his life. He had something of a religious experience in 1873 and was admitted to membership in the Columbia church. He later helped his father to edit the minutes of the General Assembly and to manage the affairs of the *North Carolina Presbyterian*—of which Dr. Wilson was editor for a time, after he accepted a call to Wilmington in 1874. "The stern

Covenanter tradition that is behind me," Woodrow
Wilson said in 1918, "sends many an echo down the
years."

A boy never gets over his boyhood (to use Wilson's
phrase), and twenty-four years of residence in the
South left deep marks. He imbibed the Southern love
of locality and adherence to State rights. He inherited
attachment to the Democratic party and a low tariff,
and shared his society's feeling of *noblesse oblige*
toward women and Negroes, along with its belief in
segregation of the races. He was proud that Southerners had taken up arms in 1861, even while he
rejoiced in the defeat of the Confederacy. He had un-
alloyed contempt for Southerners who nursed old
sectional hatreds. Like his father, he looked to a
future when the South would play a large role in
national affairs.

Education was not easy to come by during Reconstruction, and to make matters worse Tommy Wilson
was a late starter. Instruction at home and in various
private schools laid meager foundations, but he entered Davidson College, a stanchly Presbyterian institution in North Carolina, in 1873. The first year
was a struggle, made more difficult by poor health.
He left Davidson in June 1874 determined to enter
the College of New Jersey at Princeton, and he continued his studies, particularly of Greek and Latin,
at home during the next year, until he was sufficiently
prepared. He also taught himself the Graham system
of shorthand and published his first articles in the
North Carolina Presbyterian.

Princeton was a wonderful, exciting new world. He came in 1875 as Tommy Wilson, a gangling, shy, and somewhat awkward boy. He found a host of friends whose affection enriched his life to its end. He found new richness in the Reform tradition in the preaching of the college's president, James Mc-Cosh. He found a stronger national vision and purpose, for Princeton had always been a meeting ground of North and South. He discovered and carefully nurtured intellectual powers much greater than he had ever imagined he possessed. Wilson was graduated thirty-eighth in a class of 107, with an average of 90.3, but he did much more than the official record might signify. On his own he read widely and carefully in modern history, politics, and literature. He played a lively role in student affairs—in the Whig Society, of which he was Speaker; the Liberal Debating Club, which he organized; the *Princetonian,* the student newspaper, of which he was managing editor; and the baseball association, of which he was president. Most important, he discovered that his passion was politics, and he formed a "solemn covenant" with a fellow-student to "school all our powers and passions for the work of establishing the principles we held in common; that we would acquire knowledge that we might have power." His first article published in a national magazine, "Cabinet Government in the United States" (August 1879), reflected his concern over the absence of effective leadership in national affairs.

Dr. Wilson ardently wanted his son to go into the

ministry, but Woodrow (as he soon began to call himself) felt another call. He would be a statesman, a leader of men. The surest road to a political career was the law, and so he enrolled at the University of Virginia Law School in the autumn of 1879, after his graduation from Princeton. He received sound training from Professor John B. Minor, whom Wilson thought his greatest teacher next to his father. He threw himself into student activities with abandon. He also fell madly in love with a young cousin, Hattie Woodrow, who was attending the Augusta Female Seminary in Staunton. He eventually proposed, only to be somewhat unceremoniously rejected. He worked and played too hard, and a nearly complete physical collapse forced him to withdraw in early 1880. Health returned at home in Wilmington, and Wilson spent the next year and a half reading law, history, and literature—and in unsuccessful pursuit of young ladies.

Wilson felt sufficiently prepared and strong enough by the spring of 1882 to venture forth. After much hesitation, he and his father decided upon Atlanta, the booming metropolis of the New South, as the best place to practice law. Wilson arrived in June and formed a partnership with Edward I. Renick, whom he had known at the University of Virginia. Atlanta was filled with aspiring young lawyers, and Wilson had neither the disposition nor physical strength to engage in the scramble. He was admitted to the bar in October 1882, but it would be a gross exaggeration to say that he practiced law. Instead, he continued his reading, testified before the United States Tariff Commission, and wrote several articles on affairs in Georgia for the *New York Evening Post*. He also began work on a study which had taken shape in his mind after reading Walter Bagehot's *English Constitution*. It would be an analysis of the actual functioning of the American national government, and would later be expanded into his first book, *Congressional Government*.

It was not long before Wilson began to wonder whether he was in the wrong place trying to do the wrong thing. Atlanta was on the make, raw, and crude—no place for a sensitive, romantic young man. He loved too much to read and study and think large thoughts. His plain necessity, as he wrote a friend, was a profession that would give him a modest income and favorable conditions for study. How could he do better than to be a professor of politics and history? Thus he resolved in the spring of 1883 to go to graduate school, and he applied for a fellowship at the new Johns Hopkins University in Baltimore. He did not get the fellowship; no matter, he would go anyway.

Life took a happy new turn for Wilson even before Baltimore. He went to Rome, Georgia, in April 1883 on some legal business for his mother. There he met Ellen Louise Axson, daughter of the local Presbyterian minister. She loved literature and art and was uncommonly winsome and sweet. Wilson lost his heart at once but did not dare to tell her so quickly. He next saw Ellen, quite accidentally, in

Asheville in September, on his way to Baltimore.
They were both now much in love; he proposed,
and she accepted. Two days later he arrived in Baltimore.

Wilson could not have chosen a better place in
America for graduate study than the Johns Hopkins
University. He fell in with a remarkable group of
students, many of whom became distinguished teachers and scholars. He was a member of perhaps the
most famous seminar in the history of higher education in the United States, the one conducted by Professor Herbert Baxter Adams. He worked furiously,
revising chapters in his book, *Congressional Government,* and began work on a history of American economic thought with another young scholar. He
studied international law, American history, constitutional history, jurisprudence, and related subjects, as
well as German. He joined the University Glee Club
and the Hopkins Literary Society, transforming the
latter into the Hopkins House of Commons and
writing a brand-new constitution for it. Altogether,
he was a success, and he won his coveted fellowship
for a second year. Then, in January 1885, even while
he was hard at work on courses, Houghton Mifflin
published *Congressional Government.* It won enthusiastic acclaim for its perceptive analysis of the
reasons for the absence of responsible leadership in
the American constitutional system.

This was more success than the average scholar ever
achieves, but Wilson wanted more than this. He had
written about political affairs; now he wanted more

than ever "to take an active, if possible a leading, part in public life, and strike out for myself, if I had the ability, a *statesman's* career." But he wanted even more to marry Ellen Axson, and marriage meant making a living. Thus he accepted a position at the newly founded Bryn Mawr College outside Philadelphia, and he married his beloved in Savannah on June 24, 1885. The following year he took the doctor's degree at Johns Hopkins, after having resolved to avoid this final surrender to academic protocol.

Bryn Mawr was their home for the next three years. There was even more joy in marriage than Wilson had imagined, for Ellen was not only a homemaker but a delightful companion in things of the mind. Then came the blessing of parenthood, as Margaret was born on April 16, 1886, and Jessie Woodrow followed sixteen months later. A third daughter, Eleanor Randolph, born in 1889, completed the immediate family circle. Wilson plunged into work with enthusiasm. He wrote a pioneering article on public administration and began work on a textbook in comparative government, which was published in 1889 as *The State*. Even so, he stirred and kicked against the pricks. Yearning for "a seat on the inside of the government," he sought appointment as First Assistant Secretary of State. Failure to obtain the office only increased his dissatisfaction. "I love the stir of the world," he wrote. Moreover, teaching women (for Bryn Mawr was a college for women) soon began to pall on Wilson. They were, he thought, too literal and unimaginative; teaching them threat-

ened to relax his "mental muscles." "I have for a
long time been hungry for a class of *men,*" he wrote
after three years at Bryn Mawr. Finally, he never got
on well with the strong-minded dean of the college,
Miss M. Carey Thomas. He accepted a professorship
at Wesleyan University at Middletown, Connecticut,
in the spring of 1888, even though he had agreed to
continue longer at Bryn Mawr.

The Wilsons' two years in Middletown were a
happy interlude between academic apprenticeship
and achievement. They found a host of friends. Wilson was a great success as a teacher. He organized a
new student debating society, the Wesleyan House
of Commons, and helped to coach a winning football
team. In addition to his regular duties, he also began
giving a course of lectures at the Hopkins. He continued these until he assumed the presidency of
Princeton, in 1902. He also began work on a volume
in the "Epochs of American History Series," edited
by Professor Albert Bushnell Hart of Harvard. Published in 1893 under the title *Division and Reunion,*
it surveyed American political development from the
Jacksonian era through Reconstruction.

Wilson's tenure at Wesleyan was cut short in 1890
by a call from Princeton. He could not refuse the
invitation from the institution that he loved the
most; indeed, he had rather openly encouraged
friends who had been pressing his candidacy. The
Wilsons moved into a frame house at the top of what
is now Library Place, one of the loveliest streets in
Princeton. Six years later they planned and built

their own home on an adjoining lot. It was a large half-timbered house, and Wilson let the contracts and superintended construction himself, making sure that the library should be the largest room in the house!

The move to Princeton in 1890 was the beginning of twelve rich and fruitful years, when to Wilson much seemed right with a world that was very much in turmoil and change. The college—it became Princeton University in 1896—was still small and intimate, and Wilson found stimulation and warm friendship among a group of distinguished scholars. Soon he was a leader of professors in near rebellion against a do-nothing administration headed by the brilliant but indolent Francis L. Patton. Wilson's selection as the principal orator at Princeton's sesquicentennial celebration in 1896 was a striking tribute to his pre-eminence in the faculty.

He worked incredibly hard during these years. He was first of all a teacher who took his vocation seriously. To his courses in constitutional law, international law, English common law, administration, and public law he brought an infectious enthusiasm, learning, and an Olympian dignity that made a lasting impression on students. Thousands of them were sure that he was the greatest teacher they ever had, and year after year he was voted the most popular lecturer at Princeton. He continued his lectures at the Johns Hopkins, taught a course at the New York Law School in 1892, and was greatly in demand as a popular lecturer. He also wrote furiously for quality

magazines, completed *Division and Reunion,* in 1897
published a biography of George Washington, and
climaxed the period in 1902 by publishing a five-
volume *History of the American People.* Except for
Division and Reunion, none of Wilson's writing during this period was very scholarly or original. But all
of it revealed a lively intellect, a conviction that
moral purpose must infuse politics if it is to achieve
right ends, and a profoundly conservative attitude
toward political and social change.

He was, clearly, no longer a young man on the
make, but a leader of thought and academic affairs.
He was offered Adams' chair at the Johns Hopkins,
the chairmanship of the History Department at the
University of Chicago, and the presidency of several
colleges and universities, among them the University
of Illinois and the University of Virginia.

A kind of divine discontent drove Wilson to frenzied work during these years. But there were other
goads more immediate and mundane. He was without any material resources whatsoever, and Princeton
professors then had to live in an expected style. Moreover, Wilson's responsibilities went far beyond those
of his own growing family. All through the Princeton
period the Wilson house was filled with impecunious
southern relatives on both sides of the family. What
a household it was! Wilson was unquestionably lord
and master, but he ruled with love, and his family
literally worshipped him. Gay and full of fun, he
loved to rollick with children, play charades, mimic
funny people, and tell hilarious stories. And there

were many quieter moments, evenings around the fireplace, when he would read Wordsworth and Browning to the family circle.

The family was knit together in worship as well as fun. The Wilsons joined the Second Presbyterian Church in 1897, and Wilson was elected a ruling elder that same year. He moved his membership to the First Presbyterian Church in 1905, after trying vainly to persuade the members of the two churches to unite. For Wilson, faith was the way of life. Maturity found his faith unshaken by the theological storms of the late nineteenth century. He did not fit into any particular mold. Historical criticism and the evolutionary hypothesis, which he readily accepted, only strengthened his belief in revelation and the truth of scriptures. Perhaps this was true because he saw all truth in Jesus Christ and found in Him and the Holy Spirit counselors and guides through the moral complexities of life.

Chapter Two

PRINCETON: TRIUMPH AND TRIBULATION

Finishing his *History of the American People* in 1902, Woodrow Wilson longed to write the book that would give immortality to his name. He would call it *The Philosophy of Politics*. "I was forty-five three weeks ago," he wrote to Frederick Jackson Turner, the historian of the American West and his intimate friend, "and between forty-five and fifty-five, I take it, is when a man ought to do the work into which he expects to put most of himself. . . . I was born a politician and must be at the task for which, by

28

means of my historical writing, I have all these years been in training."

The "richly contemplative years," when Wilson would write a new fundamental study of politics, would remain forever a dream. Fate had other plans and purposes. Wilson was elected on June 9, 1902, to succeed Dr. Patton as president of Princeton University. Herein lies a story that can only be briefly sketched. Administration of the university had gone from bad to worse, and professors and most of the trustees were by now in open revolt, for Princeton was rapidly becoming a second-rate institution. The trustees persuaded Patton to resign by, in effect, buying his early retirement. Then they turned, apparently unanimously and without any electioneering, to Wilson. It was a matter of much comment that he was the first layman to succeed a long line of clergymen. He was inaugurated on October 25, 1902, in a gala ceremony. His inaugural address, "Princeton for the Nation's Service," was an emphatic affirmation of the need for general education.

The man who spoke on that glorious autumn day was physically striking, almost handsome in a way. He was slender and a little short of five feet eleven inches. A contemporary has left a vivid impression:

Woodrow Wilson's face is narrow and curiously geometrical. It is a rectangle, one might say, the lines are so regular. His forehead is high and his iron gray hair retreats from it somewhat, which adds to this effect. His face is refined, a face that shows breeding and family in every line, but it is heavy boned. The

cheek bones are rather high and the jaw thrusts
forward in a challenging way. The mouth is small,
sensitive, with full lips, a mouth almost too well
shaped for a man, and a woman might envy the
arched eyebrows. But the almost brutal strength of
the general bony structure of the face, and that
aggressive jaw promise an active, iron willed, fighting man. His eyes, blue-gray they looked in that
light behind his nose glasses, are very penetrating.
They have a way of narrowing when he talks that
gives him a stern, almost grim expression.

Wilson had written and spoken all his adult life
about the need for responsible leadership in government. In *Congressional Government* and elsewhere
he had contrasted the British parliamentary system,
with its fusion of executive and legislative power,
with the American presidential-congressional system, with its alleged diffusion of power. Now he
would put what he had preached into practice: he
would be Princeton's prime minister; he would lead
trustees and faculty in a general overhauling of the
university, strengthening the faculty and elevating
the work of undergraduates. He outlined what he
thought needed to be done in a report to the trustees
even before his inauguration. He asked for $6,000,-
000 for immediate needs. Of this sum, $2,250,000
would go to launch a new method of undergraduate
instruction, the preceptorial system; $1,000,000 for a
new school of science; and $2,750,000 for new pro-
fessors and buildings. He also defined his future objectives: $3,000,000 for a graduate school, $2,400,-
000 for a school of jurisprudence, $750,000 for a

school of electrical engineering, and $500,000 for a
museum of natural history.

These were bold, even breath-taking plans to transform Princeton into a first-rate university, but trustees and friends rallied behind the new leader. The
first goal, Wilson thought, had to be the preceptorial
system. It was a modification of the Oxford tutorial
system and envisaged the appointment of young professors who should serve as tutors, guides, and friends
to groups of undergraduates (precepts) in all their
upper-class studies. Fifty preceptors were to be em-
ployed to do the job. "If we could get a body of such
tutors at Princeton," Wilson told the Princeton
alumni in New York in December 1902, "we could
transform the place from a place where there are
youngsters doing tasks to a place where there are men
thinking, men who are conversing about the things
of thought."

Wilson had obtained enough money to get the
system going by the autumn of 1905. It did not work
out precisely as he had expected. Precepting undergraduates in all fields of their major studies was too
much for young scholars. Gradually the system of individual preceptors changed into one in which all
instructors and professors precepted courses in their
special fields. But there was no doubt about the over-
all success of the system. It at least provided opportunities for undergraduates to question and discuss,
rather than to learn by rote.

An integral part of Princeton's reformation was an
overhauling of curriculum and the departmental

structure. Wilson worked closely with a faculty committee during 1903–04 to achieve a fundamental reorganization. This grouped twelve departments into
four divisions, and imposed a fourfold plan of study
that required satisfaction of certain basic courses during the freshman and sophomore years (and to a
limited degree even during the last two years) and
permitted only limited concentration in specific dis-
ciplines during the junior and senior years. The plan
reflected Wilson's, indeed the entire faculty's, abhor-
rence of the free elective system and high degree of
specialization that were beginning to characterize
American undergraduate programs. Wilson and his
colleagues followed McCosh in affirming that the
main goal of a university was to produce men whose
minds had been informed and sharpened by sound
training in basic liberal studies. It was a somewhat
aristocratic concept: Princeton would try to turn out
cultured, well-rounded gentlemen, not pedants and
narrowly trained specialists.

The preceptorial system and the fourfold plan of
study were Wilson's two great visible contributions
to American higher education. They have remained
the cornerstones of the undergraduate program at
Princeton and also have been more or less copied by
many other colleges and universities. Equally, if not
more, important were the things that Wilson did
that were not so visible to the outside world. One
by-product of the preceptorial system, not entirely
unplanned, was the sudden infusion of strong new
life that came with the addition of some fifty young

teachers all at once. Wilson chose the preceptors with meticulous care. He had a keen eye for quality and an almost irresistible power to attract bright young men. Another contribution was Wilson's insistence upon high academic standards. This came out in many ways, particularly in a drastic increase in entrance requirements. "I want you to understand," Wilson once told a man who was trying to intercede for an applicant who had failed to pass the entrance examinations, "that if the angel Gabriel applied for admission to Princeton University and could not pass the entrance examinations, he would not be admitted. He would be wasting his time." Finally, Wilson insisted upon higher standards of discipline than had prevailed during Dr. Patton's casual administration. There is a story, probably authentic, that a woman whose son had just been expelled for cheating appealed to Wilson, pleading that she had to have an operation and would die if her son were not reinstated. "Madam," he replied, ". . . you force me to say a hard thing, but, if I had to choose between your life or my life or anybody's life and the good of this college, I should choose the good of the college."

So much could not be done without paying a price, for Wilson was doing more than a far from robust constitution could endure. In addition to his driving administrative work as president of the university, he continued to teach, to carry on extensive correspondence, having only a part-time secretary, and to lecture constantly. He suffered a stroke caused by arteriosclerosis in May 1906 and momentarily lost the sight of his left eye. A prominent Philadelphia specialist told him that he had to retire. Later diagnosis showed that the damage had not been so extensive. Wilson and his family left for an extended vacation in England and Scotland even before commencement. He found refreshment, as he had done several times before, in the lake district, and he returned in October full of new zest and plans for Princeton.

He explained one new plan to the trustees on December 13, 1906. It was to abolish the undergraduate eating clubs, which had grown up along Prospect Avenue since the 1870's, and to house undergraduates in quadrangles, or colleges, where they would live and eat together with faculty advisers. The trustees gave provisional approval and appointed a special committee, with Wilson at its head, to work out a plan for reorganization of campus social life. Wilson reported in June 1907 and won the authority he had requested.

Publication of the quadrangle plan on June 12, 1907, set off a storm of entirely unexpected dimension. The faculty (packed, Wilson's enemies said, with preceptors) were decisively for the project, but most of the alumni were up in arms. Their loyalty was often to the club rather than to the university. Wilson, they charged, would destroy Princeton's special character—the class and club spirit that inculcated loyalty—by mixing undergraduates of all types and classes in quadrangles. His opponents among the faculty complained bitterly that Wilson had acted

highhandedly and wrongly in asking trustee approval
without first consulting the faculty.

The storm raged unabated all through the summer and early autumn of 1907. Wilson struck back
in letters and speeches. Earlier he had accused the
clubs of undermining the "old democratic spirit" of
Princeton. This was unquestionably true: the clubs
were, unhappily, incubators of a graded social snob-
bishness. But Wilson avoided the social issue altogether in his campaign for the quadrangle plan. It
was, he must have thought, too dangerous to be used.
Instead, he concentrated on the academic issues that
he said were involved. The whole point, he said over
and over, was that the clubs were fundamentally anti-
intellectual and promoted the wrong kind of undergraduate concerns. They were side shows that were
swallowing up the main tent. Princeton had to have
a social organization the direct objective of which
was promotion of intellectual life.

The powerful alumni did not even listen, much
less understand. Their pressure was so strong (the
university was now dependent upon the gifts of a
few wealthy men among them) that the trustees sur-
rendered on October 17, 1907, and withdrew their
approval of the quadrangle plan, softening the blow
to Wilson by giving him complete freedom to agitate
for the project. He could probably have obtained a
compromise now that would have retained the clubs
but subjected them to rigorous university control—
forcing them, for example, to include all upperclass-
men. But Wilson would not compromise. Momen-

tarily so discouraged that he contemplated resigning,
he gathered courage and resolved upon a bold plan
—to appeal to his constituents, the alumni, over the
heads of his parliament, the trustees. Across the country he went intermittently between November 1907
and March 1908, appealing reasonably and in good
temper. He won some supporters in the Middle West,
but not enough to turn the tide. A trustees' committee of Wilson supporters gave the clubs a clean bill
of health in April 1908. Wilson abandoned the fight
and never publicly mentioned the quadrangle plan
again.

One reason for dropping the issue was preoccupa-
tion with a controversy over a graduate college then
just beginning. It is hard to know just when it began,
or what the real issues were. The trustees had established a graduate school in 1900 and named Andrew
Fleming West, professor of classics, as dean. West
dreamed of a Gothic establishment, like an Oxford
college, where gentlemen scholars might pursue advanced studies apart from the hurly-burly of undergraduate life. Insofar as Wilson thought about the
graduate school during the early years of his presidency, he envisaged a residential college near the
center of the campus, closely co-ordinated with undergraduate life and studies. "We shall build it," he
said in his inaugural address, "not apart, but as
nearly as may be at the very heart, the geographical
heart, of the university; and its comradeship shall be
for young men and old, for the novice as well as for
the graduate. . . . The windows of the graduate col-

lege," he added, "must open straight upon the walks and quadrangles and lecture halls of the studium generale."

Other disagreements and rivalries between West and Wilson inflated this difference over location into a first-class conflict. Both men were headstrong and determined to prevail. Jealousy arose naturally because West was, next to Wilson, the pre-eminent leader of the faculty, with his own friends among the trustees. He came out in open opposition as head of the anti-Wilson faction during the fight over the quadrangle plan. Finally, West was dedicated heart and soul to the development of a vigorous graduate program, while the graduate school was a very secondary concern to Wilson.

Smoldering antipathy had flared into mutual bitterness by the end of the quadrangle controversy. West had declined an offer of the presidency of the Massachusetts Institute of Technology in 1906, after Wilson and the trustees had promised wholehearted support for his graduate college plans. But Wilson in 1909 persuaded the trustees to reorganize the graduate school and strip West of most of his authority. Then one of West's friends among the alumni, William Cooper Procter of Cincinnati, offered $500,000 for a graduate college, provided that the trustees raise an equal sum and permit him to select the site. He would, he said, approve location on the golf links, about a mile from the center of the campus.

Everyone knew that the real issue now was control of the graduate school and college, and faculty and

trustees divided into Wilson and West factions. The
trustees voted on October 21, 1909, to accept the
Procter offer. Wilson, convinced that guidance of
university policy had been taken out of his hands,
was stunned. He laid the single, vital issue of control
squarely before the trustees. He and a majority of
the faculty, he said, had lost confidence in West; for
this reason nothing that West did could succeed. The
trustees voted on January 13, 1910, to reject the
Procter offer, but only after a violent meeting during
which Wilson lost his head and made such tactical
errors as to cause many trustees to doubt his integrity.

From this point on, the atmosphere was intolerably
tense. The West faction on the board were now
maneuvering to discredit Wilson and drive him from
office, and West was assiduously abetting their intrigues. Wilson was utterly incompetent at rough
infighting. He struck back wildly, stimulating an
editorial in *The New York Times* that said that the
controversy was really a life-and-death struggle between special privilege and democracy. In an address
before the Pittsburgh alumni on April 16, Wilson
publicly affirmed agreement with the editorial.

It was a question by this time whether the university could in fact survive. West and Wilson leaders
on the board therefore formulated a compromise,
providing for West's retirement as dean of the graduate school and location of the residential college on
the golf links, with West as resident master. Wilson
was, unhappily, in no condition to accept a compromise, even a reasonable one. He was physically ex-

hausted and emotionally distraught by the bitter conflict that had cost him some of his best friends. He rejected the compromise as, indeed, West did also. Nothing remained, it seemed, but one final battle for control of the university.

Then came a settlement, but not as anyone, except perhaps West, had anticipated. An old alumnus, Isaac C. Wyman, died on May 8, leaving his entire estate, *estimated* to be worth from $2,000,000 to $4,-000,000, to build and endow a graduate college such as West desired. "We have beaten the living," Wilson told his wife, "but we cannot fight the dead. The game is up." It was indeed. Procter renewed his offer, and the trustees accepted it on June 9. At the same meeting Wilson announced the Wyman bequest and declared that he had withdrawn his objections to construction of a graduate college on the golf links. Ironically, the Wyman estate later turned out to be worth only $600,000.

Chapter ❧ Three

THE ROAD TO THE
WHITE HOUSE

A group of men, Wilson among them, gathered at
the home of Colonel George Harvey in Deal, New
Jersey, on Sunday evening, June 26, 1910. They had
come, they told Wilson, to offer him the Democratic
nomination for the governorship of New Jersey. This,
they went on, was merely the first step in a grander
plan to put him in the White House in 1913.

Wilson was somewhat surprised but certainly not
displeased. He had continued to follow political
events closely all during the 1890's and the first dec-

40

ade of the twentieth century. He was a conservative Democrat during most of this period. He had opposed William Jennings Bryan of Nebraska and agrarian democracy in 1896; continued to profess open contempt for the Nebraskan, even though he voted for him in 1900 and 1908; and viewed the boisterous and progressive President Theodore Roosevelt with some suspicion, even though Roosevelt intrigued him greatly. The violent controversies at Princeton had caused Wilson to wonder whether those reformers who said that entrenched wealth and privilege were in mortal combat with democracy were not right, for wealth and social privilege had been his chief enemies at Princeton. But, despite this awakening consciousness, despite public demands for tariff reform and action to prevent monopoly, Wilson in 1909 and 1910 still seemed respectable and safe.

That was the main reason why the New Jersey Democratic politicians wanted him for their gubernatorial candidate in 1910. Colonel Harvey, conservative editor of *Harper's Weekly,* had suggested Wilson for the Presidency in 1906 and had tried to persuade him to be a candidate for the United States Senate in 1907. All auguries in the spring of 1910 seemed to favor launching Wilson's political career, and Harvey approached his friend James Smith, Jr., the chief leader of the New Jersey Democracy. Smith responded eagerly. Wilson, he agreed, would make a splendid governor. He could use him to head off a rebellion of young progressive Democrats that threatened to drive him from control of the state organ-

ization. Moreover, Smith delighted in the thought
that he might help to make a President of the United
States. All doubt in Smith's mind was resolved when
Wilson told a mutual friend that he as governor
would not oppose the existing Democratic organization, so long as the organization supported right policies and left him free in "the matter of measures
and men."

All this was prelude to the meeting at Harvey's
home on June 26, 1910. There never was much doubt
what Wilson's decision would be. Here was the opportunity for which he had been in training for a
lifetime. Here was a call to public service that no
Princeton man could decline. Here, indeed, was
God's own plan and purpose for his life. He expected
to win, and winning would mean release from the
mire of controversy at Princeton. His one regret was
that it would also mean abandoning friends among
the faculty and trustees and the inevitable triumph
of the West faction. But his supporters on the board
urged him on, and he told Smith and Harvey during
the first week in July that he would accept the nomination. He confirmed this decision in a letter to the
newspapers on July 15.

Wilson's announcement provoked angry accusations of intrigue and bossism from anti-machine
Democrats. They maneuvered desperately to discredit
Wilson and defeat his nomination. But Smith had
won the support of Robert Davis of Jersey City, veteran boss of the Hudson County Democratic organization, and the Smith-Davis lines held firmly against

the assault. The two leaders put Wilson's nomination across at a riotous Democratic state convention, in Trenton on September 15, by a comfortable majority. Wilson appeared, dressed in a gray sack suit, to accept the nomination and make his formal entry into the political arena. After brief preliminaries he launched a bolt of independence that set the rebellious progressives wild: "I did not seek this nomination. It has come to me absolutely unsolicited. . . . I shall enter upon the duties of the office of Governor, if elected, with absolutely no pledge of any kind to prevent me from serving the people of the State with singleness of purpose."

"Thank God, at last, a leader has come!" a young insurgent shouted.

It was true enough, as events soon proved. Wilson permitted James R. Nugent, Smith's nephew and Chairman of the Democratic State Committee, to arrange a campaign itinerary. But he chose his own counselors (the most important was Henry Eckert Alexander, editor of the *Trenton True American*) and made his own political diagnosis. It was obvious to him, as to all acute observers, that the mass of thoughtful New Jersey voters were convulsed by resentment against a Republican organization that worked hand in glove with railroads, corporations, and banks and insurance companies, and a Democratic leadership that represented the same interests, at least in Trenton. What historians call progressivism was now stirring New Jersey and other Eastern states in the same way that it had swept the

Middle West. Victory would go to the candidate who could hold the party regulars and win the discontented insurgents. The Republican nomination of a candidate tarred by too much association with his party organization gave Wilson his chance to seize control of the bipartisan reform movement and to win, even though his party was normally in the minority.

Political opportunity and necessity happily coincided with political duty for Woodrow Wilson in this, his first, campaign. After a somewhat faltering beginning he signaled his unreserved commitment, in a speech at Newark on September 30, to measures that progressives demanded: direct primaries for nomination of public officials, effective regulation of the rates and services of railroads and public utilities, and the direct election of United States senators. From this point on he drove relentlessly toward undisputed leadership of the progressive forces in a series of speeches in every county.

It was a dazzling performance, but a few of the insurgent leaders did not fail to see a certain ambiguity in the situation. Here was Wilson, passionately claiming to represent the cause of political regeneration, while stumping the state in the company of Nugent and enjoying the support of the Smith machine. The chief spokesman of Republican insurgency, George L. Record of Jersey City, decided to test Wilson's sincerity. In a public letter Record demanded to know the Democratic candidate's position on every single measure for which progressives were fighting. More to the point, he asked why Wilson denounced Republican reactionary machine politicians but ignored Democratic reactionary machine politicians.

Wilson replied on October 24, simply, forthrightly, boldly. He approved with only one slight reservation the specific measures that Record had listed. Then he frankly admitted that Smith and his colleagues were no better than Republican bosses, promised that they would be powerless if he were elected and, finally, took personal leadership of the Democratic party in the state. "That letter will elect Wilson governor," Record is reported to have said. The prediction was well founded. Wilson's letter to Record simply completed the conversion of most progressive Republicans and independents into enthusiastic Wilson supporters. Miraculously, it did not affect the loyalty of the Democratic regulars; much more than the governorship was at stake, and they had no place to go anyway. Announcement by the railroads of an increase in commuter fares just before the election helped to swell the Democratic tide on election day, November 8, 1910. Wilson carried the state by a plurality of 49,056 and helped to carry a huge Democratic majority into the lower house of the New Jersey Legislature. The Republican presidential candidate had carried the state by a majority of more than 80,000 only two years before.

Triumph came alloyed with personal bitterness and sadness for Wilson. He had apparently hoped that the Princeton trustees would wait upon the out-

come of the election to determine his future relationship to the university. The anti-Wilson faction now
firmly in control, however, somewhat brusquely demanded his resignation, and received it on October
20. The Wilsons moved from "Prospect," the president's residence on the campus, to Princeton Inn,
and then into a modest half-timbered house on Cleveland Lane which was to be their home until they
moved to the White House in 1913.

This wrenching break with the university that he
loved was followed by another personal break that
Wilson regretted but could not avoid. James Smith,
Jr., decided soon after the election that he would like
to return to the seat in the United States Senate
which he had occupied for one term in the 1890's.
Wilson was in a painful dilemma. He liked Smith
and was grateful for his support. But he could not
endorse his candidacy. He pleaded with Smith to
withdraw and suggest a compromise candidate;
Smith, confident that he had the votes, refused. Wilson was under heavy pressure from progressives, who
declared that his position on the senatorship was the
test of the sincerity of his campaign pledges. He
finally came out publicly against Smith and in support of James E. Martine, a nonentity who had run
unopposed in the Democratic senatorial preferential
primary.

Wilson knew that nothing less than his leadership
of the New Jersey Democrats and the fate of his legislative program, indeed his future political career,
were at stake in this first battle with the Smith organ-

ization. He worked furiously between November 1910 and January 1911, when the legislature, which would elect a senator, met. He rallied his supporters among assemblymen, visited Robert Davis in Jersey City, and won most of the Hudson County delegation to his side, and then pressed the campaign in statements in the newspapers and major addresses in Jersey City and Newark. It was more than Smith's weakened organization could withstand. Martine was elected on January 25, 1911, and Wilson was undisputed master of his party.

Wilson had been inaugurated meanwhile as the forty-third governor of New Jersey, on January 17, 1911. He turned to his first task—redemption of campaign pledges by the legislature—with the same deftness and vigor that he had shown in the senatorial battle. Introduction of his first major measure, the Geran bill (drafted by Record) for the nomination of party candidates in primary elections, set off a second battle with the Smith organization, one even more intense than the first. Wilson used personal pressure, cajoled, threatened, and rallied public opinion, and he pushed the Geran bill through a reluctant assembly on March 21. It was later strengthened and approved by the Senate. Adoption of the other measures that Wilson had recommended for passage by this session then followed in rapid order. A severe corrupt practices act tried to prevent fraudulent voting and bribery of public officials. A bill establishing a Public Utility Commission with ample power over rates and services was rightly regarded as one of the

most advanced of its kind in the country. A workmen's compensation bill created a state-wide system
of accident insurance. Finally, there was a measure
permitting New Jersey cities to adopt the commission
form of government. "I think . . . [the time] will
always be remembered as extraordinary in this," Wilson said in a public statement after the legislature
had adjourned, "that it witnessed the fulfillment by
the Legislature of every important campaign pledge."
"The present Legislature," Record agreed, "ends its
session with the most remarkable record of progressive legislation ever known in the political history of
this or any other State."

Wilson had little carefree time during these hectic
early months of 1911. Getting his program through
the legislature, with all that this involved, was task
enough for one man, but other pressures multiplied.
For example, he had to use his patronage powers
wisely, in order to reward his friends and lay strong
foundations for a new progressive Democratic organization. He usually followed the advice of his young
secretary, Joseph P. Tumulty of Jersey City, and
James Kerney, editor of the *Trenton Evening Times,*
but he gave careful personal attention to important
appointments, particularly administrative and judi-
cial ones. Once the legislature adjourned on April 22
he began a state-wide campaign for municipal reform
through adoption of the commission form of government. It soon turned into a fight to overthrow the
city bosses, with success in Trenton, Atlantic City,
Passaic, and a number of smaller cities. Wilson found

a few days in July for vacation with his family in Lyme, Connecticut, but he was soon back home to lead progressive Democrats in the party primary campaign. Then followed an exhausting campaign for the election of a new legislature in November. The voters returned a Republican majority in both houses, mainly because the Smith organization knifed the Democratic ticket in Essex County. "Truly, I know what 'public life' is now!" Wilson wrote during the melee. "I have no private life at all."

Nor was he likely to have much private life in the future, for he was deeply involved in a campaign for the Democratic presidential nomination by the time he penned this plaintive letter. Wilson, it will be recalled, had gone into politics with his eye on the Presidency. Remarkable circumstances were converging in the spring and summer of 1911 to make such high ambition not altogether absurd even for an utter newcomer. For one thing, the situation in the Republican camp and on the national scene was encouraging to a Democrat. The broadening reform crusades of the progressive movement had convulsed party politics ever since the late 1890's. Theodore Roosevelt, Republican President from 1901 to 1909, had led the movement in national politics and ridden the crest of the wave. His successor, William Howard Taft, was neither an enthusiastic progressive nor a skillful politician. Through a series of incredible blunders during his first year and a half in office he demonstrated his incapacity to lead, alienated progressives in his own party, and suffered a smash-

ing defeat in the congressional election of 1910. It
was obvious by 1911 that he could not hold his party
together. For another thing, the situation in the
Democratic party made the rise of a brilliant newcomer like Wilson possible. Bryan had dominated
the party for most of the period since 1896, but all
Democratic leaders and spokesmen, even Bryan's
closest friends, knew that his day was over. His announcement soon after the elections of 1910 that he
would not be a candidate for the presidential nomination in 1912 created a vacuum of leadership that
had to be filled. Fortunately for Wilson, there were
simply no veteran Democratic leaders of commanding presidential quality.

These circumstances help to explain the hopeful-
ness and expectancy with which many Democrats
looked toward New Jersey during the early months
of 1911. Wilson's campaign for the governorship, his
defeat of Smith, and above all his demonstration of
superb leadership made him the obvious and for a
time the only serious Democratic presidential hope.
He recognized his destiny and responded eagerly to
supplicating overtures. Old friends like Smith and
his type among Democratic state organizations were
friends no longer. New friends came forward in the
late winter and early spring of 1911 to form a pre-
convention campaign organization. They were, in-
terestingly, like Wilson, young Southerners living
in the North—William F. McCombs, Wilson's former
student and now a lawyer in New York; Walter H.
Page, distinguished publicist and editor of *World's*

Work; William G. McAdoo, builder of the Hudson
River tunnels; and Walter McCorkle, president of
the Southern Society of New York. They raised a
modest sum and hired a newspaper reporter to act
as Wilson's publicity agent.

The campaign organization's chief task was to cul-
tivate Democratic politicians, particularly those in
the more powerful state organizations. It was Wilson's
job to go before the country—to speak at every opportunity in order to win friends and build an irresistible mass support. He began even before the New
Jersey Legislature adjourned, with brief forays into
Georgia, Virginia, and Indiana. He met Bryan in
Princeton on March 12, and made his peace with the
man affectionately called the Great Commoner. Then
he set out on May 3 upon his first great national tour.
It carried him, as his campaign advisers had shrewdly
arranged, through the West, the home and center of
progressive Democracy. He spoke, often several times
in the same city, in Kansas City, Denver, Los Angeles,
San Francisco, Portland, Seattle, Minneapolis, St.
Paul, and Lincoln. He avoided national issues and
concentrated upon problems of state and local government. By endorsing the initiative, referendum,
and recall, commission government for cities, and the
short ballot, he left an unmistakable image of the
kind of progressive that Westerners liked. He also
plumbed popular reaction and was satisfied. On his
return home he said at last that he would run for
the Presidency, and in fact wanted to be President.
He wanted to be President, he told the reporter who

accompained him on the tour, because he wanted
the country to have a leader who would do certain
things. There were other men who could accomplish
the necessary reforms, but he was not sure that they
would carry through. "I am sure that I will at least
try to the utmost to do them."

A brief tour through the Carolinas in late May
and early June convinced Wilson that some organization was necessary to encourage and give strength to
the sentiment that was obviously rising throughout
the country. He met his friends in Washington on his
way north from South Carolina and told them that
they might establish national headquarters. Mc-
Combs, the rather self-appointed campaign manager,
opened an office in New York a short time later. By
November 1911 Wilson campaign materials were going to some 40,000 newspapers, libraries, and individuals.

It seemed during the remaining months of 1911
that nothing could prevent Wilson's triumph at the
Democratic national convention in 1912. By speaking out forthrightly on national issues like the
"Money Trust" he had won the support of virtually
all the progressive Democratic factions in the East
and South, then battling for control of their state
organizations. Pennsylvania and Texas, where these
progressives predominated, were securely won by
autumn. On the other hand, he had also aroused the
anger of the conservative press and raised grave sus-
picions among more moderate observers that he was
"Bryanizing," that is, that he was, as one newspaper

said, "preparing with his initiative, referendum and recall programme and his money-trust bugaboo to swallow Mr. Bryan's entire Confession of Faith."

This was merely a rumbling prelude to a wholesale attack, a combination of intrigues and open assaults, aimed at destroying the new progressive leader. The New York *Sun,* the high priest of Eastern conservatism, led the way by revealing that Wilson had applied for a Carnegie pension after resigning the presidency of Princeton. Then it published on January 8, 1912, a letter that Wilson had written in 1907 expressing the wish that something might be done "to knock Mr. Bryan once for all into a cocked hat!" Colonel Harvey soon afterward announced in *Harper's Weekly* that he had taken Wilson's name from the magazine's masthead because Wilson had said that its support was hurting his candidacy. The implication of ingratitude was obvious. What hurt Wilson's cause more, indeed nearly wrecked it, was the disclosure by William Randolph Hearst and his network of newspapers that Wilson had earlier condemned labor unions and slurred immigrants from southern and eastern Europe.

Three other Democratic presidential contenders —Champ Clark of Missouri, Oscar W. Underwood of Alabama, and Judson Harmon of Ohio—had meanwhile entered the field. They surged forward while Wilson reeled under the massive attack. Clark, Speaker of the House of Representatives, was a veteran Bryanite with a strong progressive record and no qualifications for national leadership. Underwood,

Chairman of the Ways and Means Committee of the
House, enjoyed some national reputation as the
Democratic party's chief expert on tariff reform.
Harmon, Governor of Ohio, made an open bid for
conservative support and never developed any popular following. While Clark inherited Bryan's following in the West and made expedient alliances with
state organizations in the Middle West and East,
Underwood won about one hundred delegates in the
South, who would probably have gone to Wilson had
the Alabamian not been a candidate. It seemed almost certain by the end of May 1912 that the Wilson
movement had collapsed. "What we now look forward to with not a little dread," Wilson wrote on
June 17, "are the possibilities of the next fortnight
in politics." He and his family had moved two days
before to the Governor's Cottage at Sea Girt on the
Jersey coast.

Exactly ten days later, on June 25, Democratic
leaders and delegates descended on Baltimore for the
opening of the party's national convention. There
was no doubt by this time what the chief issue was:
whether the party would nominate a vigorous progressive free to serve the country, or a party hack
bound by entangling alliances. It was made clear
enough for even the blind to see during a spirited
battle between Bryan and Alton B. Parker, a New
York conservative, for the temporary chairmanship
of the convention. Wilson supported Bryan. Clark
tried to dodge, then supported Parker.

Wilson had principles, but Clark had the votes,

440½ of them on the first ballot, as compared with Wilson's 324, Harmon's 148, Underwood's 117½, and a scattering given to favorite sons. There was a good deal of sparring and little change during the first nine ballots. Then the Tammany chieftains swung New York's ninety votes to Clark on the tenth ballot, giving him well over a majority, but not the two thirds then necessary for a Democratic presidential nomination. Clark, in Washington, wrote out a telegram of acceptance; Wilson, in Sea Girt, sent a telegram to McCombs authorizing him to release his delegates.

But Wilson's managers and delegates in Baltimore stood firm. More important, they made an alliance with Underwood's managers so ironclad that they could block Clark's nomination forever. It was not so easy to find a two-thirds majority for Wilson. Bryan, a delegate from Nebraska, switched his vote from Clark to Wilson on the fourteenth ballot. This brought new moral support but few votes. Wilson's greatest strength lay in the lukewarmness of the Speaker's support and in the growing conviction that only Wilson could win the Presidency. His managers ate away at Clark's strength skillfully during the ensuing grueling ballots. Wilson finally passed Clark on the thirtieth ballot, on July 1. He achieved a majority on the forty-second ballot, on the following day, when Illinois deserted Clark, and the necessary two thirds on the forty-sixth ballot, when the Underwood delegates came into the Wilson camp in order to prevent a deadlock. Wilson wanted Under-

wood for his running mate, but the Alabamian refused, and the vice-presidential nomination went to
Governor Thomas R. Marshall of Indiana.

The telegraph key clicked out the news at Sea
Girt, and a brass band and a crowd of well-wishers
signalized the victory. Democrats had good cause for
cheer. They had not been accustomed to winning
presidential elections since 1892, or even to thinking
that they had a chance to win since 1896. Events of
June and early July 1912 had wrought remarkable
changes. The Republican party had been racked
by a bitter contest for the presidential nomination
between President Taft and Theodore Roosevelt.
Taft had won a narrow victory at the cost of dis-
rupting his party. The Roosevelt delegates had
stormed out of the Republican convention in Chicago, and their hero had issued a call for a third
party, the Progressive party, and announced that he
would run at the head of its ticket.

Wilson did not miss the significance of events in
Chicago, but he had little time to contemplate the
future in happy expectation. He was overwhelmed
at Sea Girt by a flood of letters and an unrelenting
stream of visitors—friends, former enemies, the entire Democratic National Committee, and others.
"You cannot . . . imagine such days . . . an invasion
by the people of the United States," he wrote on
July 6. "The life I am leading now *can't* keep up,"
he wrote a week later. "It is inconceivable that it
should. I wish I could describe it to you, but I fear
it is as indescribable as it is inconceivable. Not a

moment am I left free to do what I would. I thought last night that I should go crazy with the strain and confusion of it."

The most immediate problems were appointment of a national Democratic chairman and formation of a campaign organization. Wilson finally named McCombs as national chairman, even though he did not really like or trust him and would have preferred McAdoo. McCombs was domineering, irascible, and intensely jealous of anyone close to Wilson. Never strong physically, he broke completely under the strain and left headquarters in McAdoo's charge.

The details of running a gigantic campaign were of course beyond Wilson's concern. His task was more important, and in fact more difficult. It was to convince the country that the Democratic party, which had so long been torn by quarrels between its agrarian and urban factions and was still blighted with the stigma of sectionalism, could be a responsible vehicle of national government. He also had to prove that he, Wilson, could lead in the great presidential tradition. The task was all the more urgent because the voters had an attractive alternative: not in Taft, who knew that he was beaten and made no fight, nor in Eugene V. Debs, the Socialist candidate who campaigned as if he had a chance, but in Theodore Roosevelt. Roosevelt's smile was alone worth a million votes. More important, he campaigned on a platform, adopted by the Progressive national convention in early August, that embodied much of the advanced progressive thought of the time. (Roosevelt called his program the New Nationalism. It included all the stock proposals for political reform, such as the direct election of United States senators, woman suffrage, and presidential preferential primaries. To advanced reformers, particularly social workers and champions of the Social Gospel, the most exciting provisions were for far-reaching economic and social reform by *national regulation of industry, business, and working* conditions and wages.

Wilson opened his campaign with an acceptance speech from the front porch of the Governor's Cottage on August 7. He discussed the Democratic platform (which Bryan had largely dictated) in a grave and dignified way, endorsing its demands for tariff reform, more stringent legislation against monopolies, and measures to encourage organized labor. In addition, he promised "an unentangled government, a government that cannot be used for private purposes."

The great audience applauded politely, but the effort did not stir excitement as Roosevelt's acceptance speech, his "Confession of Faith," had recently done. Nor did Wilson make much impact in three subsequent addresses in New Jersey, when he emphasized the somewhat threadbare themes of tariff reform and disinterested government. He seemed to be stumbling; actually, he was searching for the single great issue, the one that would give meaning to all the others. He found it during a conference on August 28 with Louis D. Brandeis, the "people's attorney" of Boston and probably the outstanding authority in the country on large economic problems. Brandeis gave Wilson a program, the restoration of competition and unleashing of economic energies by the regulation of competition itself. This Wilson later called, in its more elaborate form, the New Freedom for "the man who is knocking and fighting at the closed doors of opportunity."

From this point on, the country was treated to the most instructive and fundamental political debate since the Lincoln-Douglas debates of 1858. Roosevelt pressed his campaign for national reconstruction with mounting force and popular response. Wilson responded with speeches that grew in intensity as the weeks passed. He had no quarrel, he said, with Roosevelt's proposals for social and economic reform and a square deal for the common man. The trouble was that Roosevelt wanted to legalize monopolies and entrust the fate of the common man to an all-powerful national government that would be controlled by big business itself. "I want to fight for the liberation of America," Wilson cried out at Scranton on September 23. He was not making a campaign against individuals, he declared in Denver on October 7, at the height of a Western tour. It was a "crusade against powers that have governed us—that have limited our development—that have determined our lives—that have set us in a straitjacket to do as they please. This is a second struggle for emancipation. . . . If America is not to have free enterprise, then she can have freedom of no sort whatever."

The campaign's pace was severe, but Wilson loved the crowds and actually seemed to thrive upon the physical rigors. "I keep singularly well," he wrote to a friend in early September. "I've gained seven pounds and a half since I was nominated. . . . If my days are trying and so full of—everything that fatigues and distracts—as to make them quite overwhelming, they at least fly fast with satisfactory rapidity." He was also deeply moved by the warmth and affection of the common people; they nearly overwhelmed him on his Western tour in October. He returned to the East for a brilliant series of speeches, climaxed by a great effort in Madison Square Garden in New York City on October 31.

Wilson was at home on election day, November 5, 1912, enjoying the intimacy of a family circle enlarged by numerous kinsmen. McAdoo and other friends came down from New York in the afternoon. They had dinner and good conversation and then gathered in the living room for the election returns. Mrs. Wilson carried the formal announcement of his election to her husband at about ten o'clock. There was not much cause for personal pride once all the returns were in. Wilson won a smashing victory in the Electoral College because of the division in the Republican vote; and the Democrats would have good majorities in both houses of Congress for the same reason. But Wilson polled only 42 per cent of the popular votes, fewer in number, actually, than Bryan had polled in 1908.

The bell in Nassau Hall rang, and Princeton students and townspeople began to gather with torches and flags in Cleveland Lane. Wilson came out to acknowledge their ovations. Standing on a chair, he said:

> Gentlemen, I am sincerely glad to see you. I can't help thinking this evening that something has only begun which you will have a great part in carrying forward. There is so much to reconstruct and the reconstruction must be undertaken so justly and by slow process of common counsel, that a generation or two must work out the result to be achieved. . . . I summon you for the rest of your lives to work to set this government forward by processes of justice, equity and fairness. I myself have no feeling of triumph tonight. I have a feeling of solemn responsibility.

Chapter Four

THE NEW FREEDOM

"I am through with statements," Wilson told reporters on the day after his election to the Presidency.
"I am now going to do some hard thinking." This
was easier said than done during the confusion of
the days that followed. "Our little house was a ter-
rible mess," Wilson's daughter remembered, "and
mother, for the first and only time in her life, walked
through rooms pretending that she didn't see the
confusion and disorder." Wilson needed time to rest
and think about the tasks ahead. "I find myself, after
two years of continuous strain, rather completely
fagged out," he explained. Inevitably his thoughts

turned toward Bermuda, where he had often found refuge before. He sailed with his family on November 16, 1912, and returned a month later, a new man. "We all feel ready for anything," he told reporters when his ship docked in New York on December 16.

The first task was construction of a new Administration, from local postmasters to Cabinet members and ambassadors, from the ground up and from a party not then blessed with an abundance of talent. Wilson in choosing his Cabinet relied most heavily upon the advice of Colonel Edward M. House of Texas, a winning man who gave the impression of entire altruism and wisdom. He had met Wilson only a year before and played a minor role in the pre-convention and presidential campaigns. Wilson liked and trusted him because he seemed to want nothing for himself.

There never was much doubt that the position of Secretary of State had to go to Bryan, still the leader of agrarian Democrats, whose support for legislative measures would be indispensable. Wilson offered him the post with a show of pleasure on December 21. For Secretary of the Treasury, Wilson turned to McAdoo, who had won his heart as well as his admiration. No appointment was more crucial than choice of an Attorney General. Wilson wanted Brandeis, but he yielded to the protests of businessmen and Massachusetts Democrats and named James C. McReynolds of Tennessee, a former Assistant Attorney General, on House's recommendation. Wilson

appointed McReynolds to the Supreme Court in
1914, chiefly to get him out of the Cabinet, and
named the more congenial and progressive Thomas
Watt Gregory of Texas to his post. Josephus Daniels,
editor of the Raleigh *News and Observer,* became
the Secretary of the Navy as reward for his great help
during the preconvention campaign. To head the
Interior Department there was Franklin K. Lane
of California, who did not altogether share the West's
desire for rapid distribution of the public domain.
Organized labor's choice for Secretary of Labor was
William B. Wilson, former secretary-treasurer of the
United Mine Workers and congressman from Pennsylvania. The President-elect called him gladly. To
House's old friends, David F. Houston, chancellor
of Washington University in St. Louis, and Albert
S. Burleson, congressman from Texas, went the
posts of Secretary of Agriculture and Postmaster General. Joseph P. Tumulty, whom Wilson retained as
his secretary, found at the last minute in Lindley M.
Garrison, a New Jersey judge, someone who would
serve as Secretary of War. Garrison resigned in 1916
and was replaced by Newton D. Baker, Mayor of
Cleveland. Wilson thought again of Brandeis for
Secretary of Commerce but yielded under pressure
and named William C. Redfield, a New York congressman. Membership in the Cabinet was never
able to raise him from obscurity. It was not a distinguished Cabinet, but it was broadly representative
of the country, and it was the best that Wilson could
find.

There was, besides, unfinished business in New Jersey to be completed before going to Washington. The Democrats had regained control of the legislature, and Wilson was determined to climax his governorship by adoption of stringent antitrust legislation and a bill to reform New Jersey's antiquated and corruption-ridden jury system. He won his antitrust bills, known as the Seven Sisters, without difficulty, but nothing he could do, not even an appeal to the people, could force the jury reform bill over the opposition of the city machines.

Now the days in Princeton, that village of his youth and manhood, that home of sad and bitter memories, were drawing to a close. A great throng of friends came to say good-by, and Wilson and his wife walked from Cleveland Lane to the special train that was waiting to take them and a crowd of Princeton students to Washington. Chief Justice Edward D. White administered the oath to the twenty-eighth President of the United States in the inaugural rituals on March 4, 1913. Turning from the Chief Justice, Wilson noticed that the police had cleared a large area in front of the inaugural stand on the east front of the Capitol. "Let the people come forward," he said. Then he began his inaugural address by announcing simply, "There has been a change of government." He ended in a burst of prayerful cadence:

> The Nation has been deeply stirred, stirred by a solemn passion, stirred by the knowledge of wrong, of ideals lost, of government too often debauched and made an instrument of evil. The feelings with

which we face this new age of right and opportunity
sweep across our heartstrings like some air out of
God's own presence, where justice and mercy are
reconciled and the judge and the brother are one.
We know our task to be no mere task of politics but
a task which shall search us through and through,
whether we be able to understand our time and the
need of our people, whether we be indeed their
spokesmen and interpreters, whether we have the
pure heart to comprehend and the rectified will to
choose our high course of action.

This is not a day of triumph; it is a day of dedica-
tion. Here muster, not the forces of party, but the
forces of humanity. Men's hearts wait upon us; men's
lives hang in the balance; men's hopes call upon us
to say what we will do. Who shall live up to the great
trust? Who dares fail to try? I summon all honest
men, all patriotic, all forward-looking men, to my
side. God helping me, I will not fail them, if they
will but counsel and sustain me!

Life in the White House was certainly different
from the unpretentious routine of daily life in Princeton. It was strange to have a corps of servants and
several automobiles. It was irritating to be always
the center of attention and to be unable to walk
when and where one pleased. Yet personal life
changed fundamentally very little for the Wilsons.
Mrs. Wilson entertained when she had to, but she
had no interest in society and gave herself as she had
always done to her family and quiet works of charity.
The Wilsons moved their membership to Central
Presbyterian Church of Washington and worshipped
there as regularly and unobtrusively as they could.

Routine was broken by a summer vacation at Cornish, New Hampshire, in 1913 and by a brief trip to Pass Christian, Mississippi, in late December 1913 and early January 1914. There were also festive times in the White House, when Jessie Wilson married Francis B. Sayre on November 25, 1913, and Eleanor married McAdoo on May 7, 1914.

Not even the White House could alter Wilson's ingrained habit of living and working according to a nearly inflexible routine. On many mornings he rose early to play golf before going to his office. He read his mail and dictated letters from nine to ten in the morning. Then he received visitors or held Cabinet meetings until about one o'clock. He returned to his office after lunch for more appointments and work between two and four o'clock. Then followed golf with his physician, Cary T. Grayson, or an automobile ride with Mrs. Wilson and Grayson. Dinner was at seven, followed, when circumstances permitted, by conversation in the drawing room. As time passed Wilson more and more had to go to his office and work late into the night.

He worked incredibly hard and probably carried heavier burdens than any previous President. He delegated as much authority as he could to his Cabinet members and worked in almost complete harmony with them. But he was chiefly responsible for legislative policies and relations with Congress, and he was compelled increasingly to conduct the foreign relations of the United States and even to draft important diplomatic correspondence. He wrote all his own speeches and press statements and a large portion of his important correspondence on his own typewriter. His method was to draft the speech or letter in his Graham shorthand, then to transcribe it himself on his portable typewriter. These duties and many others he performed with virtually no staff, except for stenographers and the indispensable Tumulty, who was his chief press officer and a valuable liaison with Democratic politicians.

The opportunities for leadership in 1913 were, if anything, greater than the burdens of doing the business of the Presidency. To begin with, circumstances permitted Wilson virtually to shape and form a new Democratic party. That party between Reconstruction and Wilson's inauguration had been not much more than a Southern organization with strong allies in the big-city machines of the East and Middle West and weak support in the rural and mining states of the West. Democrats, out of control of Congress after 1895 and of the White House after 1897, had been torn by sectional and personal dissensions and had failed generally to attract support among the urban middle classes and professional groups. Wilson used his vast patronage to build a new Democratic party of forward-looking young progressives. It was not always possible to do everything that he wanted to do because senatorial privilege prevented him from directly challenging senators who represented entrenched machines. But Wilson used his appointive power where he could, in states like New York, Pennsylvania, Ohio, and Wisconsin,

to lay foundations for the Democracy of the New
Deal era.

Great, too, were the opportunities for larger leadership in the slow reconstruction of national policies
and life. There could be no doubt that the great majority of thoughtful people in both parties, agitated
and made apprehensive by muckrakers, reformers,
and demagogues, desperately wanted a fundamental
overhauling. The progressive movement was at high
tide, and it was Wilson's great fortune to come to
leadership in Washington, as he had in Trenton, at
a time of culmination. His was the task of channeling
discontent into constructive channels and of laying
foundations for a political economy that could grapple with the problems of a new age.

He was superbly equipped both in theory and in
practice. He was deeply immersed in the humani-
tarian, democratic traditions of Great Britain and
his own country. He knew the American people—
their basic decency, altruism, and patriotism—and
he spoke language that, to use Lincoln's phrase,
stirred mystic chords of memory. He was a spellbinder
during a period when the American people still
treasured oratory. But he used his powers to appeal
to men's minds and spirits, not to their baser passions.

In the American constitutional system the President proposes but Congress often disposes in matters
of legislative policy. Wilson, again because of remarkable circumstances, had the opportunity to re-
veal what marvelous powers of legislative leadership

usually lie dormant in the presidential office. There
were no rival party leaders in Congress to thwart his
purposes. Nearly half the Democratic congressmen
in 1913 had been elected for the first time the year
before. They wanted patronage and re-election and
eagerly followed Wilson's lead. But so also did most
of the veterans, for they knew that the fate of their
party depended upon satisfaction of the popular
demand for change.

Wilson took party leadership in Congress simply
by asserting it boldly. Even before he went to Washington he conferred with Democratic leaders about
the general outlines of a legislative program. In
Washington he gave close attention to preparation
of bills, conferred frequently at the Capitol and in
the White House, synthesized and reconciled oppos-
ing points of view, and personally guided legislation
from committee to final approval. What made him
usually irresistible was his fusion of the powers of
the Presidency with those of party leader, along with
intense moral purpose. "We always come away,"
one congressman said, "feeling that we have been
convinced, not by Mr. Wilson—certainly not driven
or bossed by him—but with the feeling that we are
all—President, Congress, and people—in the presence
of an irresistible situation. Here are the facts, he
says; here are the principles, here are our obligations
as Democrats. What are we going to do about it?
He has a curious way of making one feel that he,
along with all of us, is perfectly helpless before the
facts in the case."

But for what objectives should such enlivened power be used? Wilson at the outset thought that the answer was fairly simple. He would try, of course, to administer the government honestly, without favor to individuals or classes. Then legislation would bring the New Freedom by three fundamental reforms: drastic tariff reductions, to make American producers more efficient and give consumers the benefit of competitive prices: revision of the country's antiquated banking and currency laws, in order to offset Wall Street's power by building new financial centers and opening channels of credit to small businessmen; and strengthening of the Sherman Antitrust Act in such a way as to safeguard competition without creating a gigantic engine of national economic power. This, Wilson believed, would encourage private enterprise and individual energies without launching the federal government into the kind of direct participation in economic decisions that Roosevelt's New Nationalism had envisaged.

Tariff revision came first, because the Republicans had outraged the country by adopting the Aldrich-Payne Tariff Act of 1909, and the Democrats had made it the chief issue since that date. Wilson, on March 17, called Congress into special session for April 7. He broke the custom established by Jefferson and appeared in person before a joint session on April 8 to ask for abolition of all tariff rates that bore "even the semblance of privilege or of any kind of artificial advantage."

The appearance before Congress electrified the

country (Wilson also enjoyed the thought that he had "put something over" on the master showman, Roosevelt!) and focused national attention on Capitol Hill, as Wilson had intended. He needed all the help that an aroused public opinion could muster. The measure that Chairman Underwood of the Ways and Means Committee pushed through the House of Representatives on May 8 gave free entry to clothing, boots and shoes, steel and steel products, and a number of other items, and it reduced the average tariff rates on dutiable products from about 40 per cent to 29 per cent. It also included provision for a modest income tax—the first under the Sixteenth Amendment, which had been ratified only two months before. Most important, it put sugar and wool on the free list, as Wilson had sternly insisted.

That was the rub. More accurately, it was the source of danger to Wilson's leadership. It was easy enough to steam-roller the Underwood bill through a pliant House of Representatives. But the Democrats had a majority of only six in the Senate, and free sugar and wool had alienated at least five Democratic senators from Louisiana and the West. By combining with the Republicans they could wreck not only tariff reform but the new Administration as well, as Westerners had done quite handily in 1894 and 1909. Senators from the wool and sugar states in 1913 were under heavy pressure from constituents, and more immediately, a horde of lobbyists pleading for special interests.

Wilson, profoundly disturbed, conferred with

wavering senators. When rumors circulated that he would compromise, he told reporters testily, "When you get a chance, just say that I am not the kind that considers compromises when I once take my position. Just note that down so that there will be nothing more of that sort transmitted to the press." Then, on May 26, he issued a public statement denouncing the "industrious" and "insidious" tariff lobby. "It is of serious interest to the country," he said, "that the people at large should have no lobby and be voiceless in these matters, while great bodies of astute men seek to create an artificial opinion and to overcome the interests of the public for their private profit."

The shot hit home, with more telling effect than Wilson could have hoped for. Republican senators, in a move to embarrass the President, proposed a special committee to investigate the alleged lobby. The Democrats agreed but added the stipulation that senators should disclose their property holdings or financial interests that might be affected by tariff legislation. The investigation revealed a powerful lobby that had spent millions of dollars to defeat free sugar. It also focused attention on senators personally at the very moment that debate on the Underwood bill was beginning in the upper house.

The result showed what courageous leadership could accomplish. The Senate increased the income tax and actually lowered many of the Underwood rates, bringing the general average of the tariff bill down to approximately 26 per cent. "I feel to-night," Wilson said as he signed the bill on October 3, 1913, "like a man who is lodging happily in the inn which lies half way along the journey, and that in the morning, with a fresh impulse, we shall go the rest of the journey, and sleep at the journey's end like men with a quiet conscience, knowing that we have served our fellowmen, and have thereby tried to serve God."

Victory in the tariff battle, as one London editor said, raised Wilson "at a single stage from the man of promise to the man of achievement." It also confirmed his supremacy as party leader in the midst of a more difficult and important struggle for currency and banking reform. No one who knew anything about the subject doubted that the need was dire. The national banking structure, established in 1863–64, was about as badly adapted to the financial needs of a great nation as any system could have been. It provided only a primitive reserve system, and no effective method of mobilizing or shifting reserves in times of crisis. Its currency was based in large part on the bonded indebtedness of the United States and bore no direct relation to business and agricultural production and need. A sharp bankers' panic in 1907 had exposed these weaknesses and prompted appointment of a National Monetary Commission, headed by Senator Nelson W. Aldrich of Rhode Island, to investigate and recommend. It proposed creation of a gigantic central reserve bank with fifteen branches, to be owned and controlled by banks participating in the new system.

To Democrats this sounded suspiciously like legalizing the "Money Trust," that far-flung financial

combination whose nerve center was J. P. Morgan &
Company. But Democrats were fearfully divided in
1913, as they had been since the 1890's, over the
question of the role that the federal government
should play. One group represented small-city bankers who were an important element in the urban progressive movement. Their spokesman, Carter Glass
of Virginia, Chairman of the House Banking and
Currency Committee, drafted a bill creating a thoroughly decentralized reserve system but providing
private control of the reserve banks and new currency. Wilson saw the measure's weakness and insisted upon addition of a central board to co-ordinate
the system and perform the functions of a central
reserve bank. Thus amended, the Glass bill was submitted to Democratic leaders in early May 1913. It
provoked the opposition of a second and larger
Democratic faction in Congress, the Bryanites. They
did not object to a decentralized reserve system, but
as Bryan made clear, they would approve nothing less
than exclusive public control of the central reserve
board and governmental issue of and liability for the
new currency.

Wilson broke the impasse by yielding to Bryan's
demand, in part because Brandeis convinced him that
Bryan was right, in part because he had no alternative
if he wanted any banking legislation at all. Thus a
banking and currency bill revised to merit Bryan's
public approval went to the House Banking and
Currency Committee on July 8, 1913. It set off savage
opposition from yet another Democratic faction,

Southern and Western agrarians in the Populist tradition. They condemned the measure, now called
the Federal Reserve bill, because it aimed no direct
blows at the so-called Money Trust, permitted private control of the reserve banks (and in actual fact
the money supply), and made no explicit provision
for agricultural credits. Wilson, assisted in the crucial
stages by Bryan, met this attack by compromise. He
promised action against the "Money Trust" in forth-
coming antitrust legislation, and he approved a provision for extension of short-term agricultural credits
in the Federal Reserve bill. The Democrats, finally
united by Wilson's mediation, pushed the measure
through the House of Representatives on September 18.

More dangerous difficulties lay ahead. Organized
bankers, the most powerful single economic group
in the country, were up in arms, denouncing the
Federal Reserve bill as socialistic because it vested
control over vital economic policies in a presiden-
tially appointed Federal Reserve Board. Wilson tried
to find common ground with the bankers, but they
were so extreme in opposition that he had no alternative but to fight it out. The struggle concentrated
in the Senate, where most Republicans took the
bankers' point of view. The controversy was long and
harrowing, but Wilson kept control of both his temper and his Senate followers. Opinion in the country
at large gradually but massively turned to the President's side, and the Senate approved the bill on December 19. Wilson signed the measure in a festive

ceremony at the White House on December 23. It
was his crowning domestic achievement.

Antitrust legislation to complete the New Freedom
program at first seemed easier to achieve, but its way,
too, was filled with hidden obstacles. Wilson appeared before a joint session of Congress on January
20, 1914, to explain his broad purposes. The antagonism between government and business was over,
he said, and Congress could now proceed "in quiet
moderation" to write "the additional articles of our
constitution of peace, the peace that is honor and
freedom and prosperity." Those articles were embodied in a series of bills that he and Democratic
leaders worked out during the ensuing weeks. The
first, introduced by Representative Henry D. Clayton
of Alabama, was Wilson's main answer to the so-
called trust problem. It tightened the Sherman Antitrust Act by enumerating and outlawing a number of
unfair trade practices and interlocking arrangements
that had been the chief tools of monopolists. A second
measure, sponsored by Representative James H.
Covington of Maryland, created an independent Interstate Trade Commission with power to investigate
and recommend, but not to take action on its own
initiative to prevent restraint of trade. A third measure, prepared by Representative Sam Rayburn of
Texas, gave the Interstate Commerce Commission
authority over issuance of new securities by the railroads.

Opposition came first from Wilson's friends, from
leaders of the American Federation of Labor and

their spokesmen in Congress. They threatened to
wreck the Clayton bill because it included no provisions to give labor unions immunity from prosecution
under the Sherman Act for practices (like secondary boycotts and black lists) which federal courts
had deemed to be illegal restraints of trade. There
were angry conferences at the White House, but Wilson would not yield the essential demand, even
though he did approve inclusion in the Clayton bill
of a sop that won labor's grudging acquiescence. It
declared that labor unions were not, in themselves,
combinations in restraint of trade. Thus amended,
the Clayton bill, in company with the Covington and
Rayburn bills, passed the House of Representatives
on June 5, 1914.

Ensuing debates in the Senate revealed deep fis-
sures in what to this point had seemed to be a solid
progressive front. To begin with, the great mass of
small businessmen complained that the Clayton bill's
severe provisions would prevent the very kind of
co-operation that they needed to perfect if they were
to survive. More important, a bipartisan progressive
coalition in the Senate argued that it was impossible
to define all possible forms of restraint of trade, as
the Clayton bill tried to do. The surest way to preserve competition, they said, was to outlaw restraint
of trade in sweeping fashion and then to create a
trade commission with full power to supervise day-
to-day activities in the business world. Brandeis,
Wilson's chief mentor on antitrust matters, had also
been converted to this point of view. One of his

friends, Raymond B. Stevens of New Hampshire, introduced a bill for a strong Federal Trade Commission at the height of the impasse in the Senate.

Some hard thought and further conversation with Brandeis convinced Wilson that his progressive critics were right. At his prompting the Senate Commerce Committee eagerly incorporated the heart of the Stevens plan into a new Federal Trade Commission bill, and a bipartisan coalition pushed it through the Senate on August 5 and the House on September 10. Wilson had meanwhile lost interest in the Clayton bill. Cut adrift, its severe provisions were gravely weakened by amendments in the Senate, and Wilson signed it without comment on October 15. The Rayburn bill died in the Senate, a victim mainly of the disorganization of the security markets that followed the outbreak of war in Europe in the summer of 1914.

Observers, looking back in the autumn of 1914 over events since Wilson's inauguration, were quick to see the differences between the New Freedom promised and the New Freedom embodied in legislation on the statute books. Wilson had moved, under the pressure of new convictions and political necessity, a good distance away from the somewhat doctrinaire liberalism of 1912 toward a more dynamic progressive nationalism. The modest beginning of a new democratic tax policy, inaugurated by the income tax provisions of the Underwood Act, the provisions for federal direction if not control of banking and monetary policies in the Federal Reserve

Act, and adoption of a quasi-Rooseveltian solution
to the trust problem all testified to an important
movement, not merely in Wilson's thought, but in
the main direction of American progressivism in
general.

It was impossible to say whether the progressive
movement would drive further away from laissez
faire toward the active, regulating national state.
Well-organized groups were already hard at work to
speed the momentum leftward. Social reformers were
demanding a federal child labor law and other measures for social justice. Farmers wanted the government to open land banks to provide long-term rural
credit. Church leaders were now pressing for federal
legislation against Demon Rum. Women, particularly in the West and North, were demanding a
federal woman-suffrage amendment.

To these and other such proposals Wilson replied
either with open opposition or by refusal to give
crucial support. It was not that he usually disap-
proved the objectives of advanced reformers, although
in one instance—his condoning of a limited segregation in some departments in Washington—he did out-
rage humanitarians and Negroes. It was, rather, that
he could not conscientiously approve class and spe-
cial-interest legislation, like federal rural credits, or
measures, such as a federal child labor bill, that
would invade the right of the states to control domestic relationships. He gave his answer to impatient
reformers in a public letter addressed to Secretary
McAdoo in November 1914: The progressive move-

ment had found fulfillment in the three great New Freedom measures; he had finished the work that he set out to do in March 1913; reform was over.

The writing of this letter found Wilson, much against his will, deeply involved in diplomatic problems of the highest order of urgency. It had been so from the outset of his term, even though he had no preparation for the conduct of foreign affairs and, at least in the beginning, little interest in the outside world.

Wilson and Secretary of State Bryan came into office in 1913 with hopeful if limited expectations for foreign policy. They would maintain traditional isolation from European politics, abandon Taft's "dollar diplomacy" (use of American private financial resources to reinforce diplomatic policies) in China and Latin America, and try to lead the world to peace by moral example. To some degree they achieved these objectives. Bryan persuaded thirty governments to sign "cooling off" treaties—providing for investigation of disputes that might lead to war—with the United States in 1913-14. Wilson, with the Secretary's approval, withdrew support from an international banking consortium that had been formed to lend money on dubious terms to China. Moreover, he granted early diplomatic recognition to the struggling Chinese Republic in 1913 and came somewhat aggressively, but certainly effectively, to its rescue in 1915, when Japan tried to impose certain demands that would have transformed China into her satellite. Bryan negotiated a treaty of reparation with Colom-

bia, offering apology and indemnity for Roosevelt's
alleged aggression in the Colombian province of
Panama in 1903. It helped to restore American moral
standing even though the Senate refused to give its
consent to ratification. Wilson, almost single-handed,
forced Congress in the spring of 1914 to repeal the
provision of the Panama Canal Act of 1912 exempting American coastwise ships using the canal from
payment of tolls, on the ground that the exemption
violated the Hay-Pauncefote Treaty of 1901 with
Great Britain. Except for the Far Eastern crisis of
1915 set off by Japan's demands on China, these were
all uncomplicated episodes, success in which depended largely on what men in Washington did.

It was not so easy to practice a moral foreign policy
or to achieve one's goals when dangerous emotions
and vital interests were involved. A good example
was the controversy with Japan provoked in 1913
when the California legislature took action to forbid
Japanese subjects from owning farm land in the
state. Californians quite frankly admitted that racial
antipathy and determination to discriminate moti-
vated them. Wilson shared their anti-Japanese prejudices, but he tried to persuade Californians to avoid
an invidious discrimination and even sent Bryan to
Sacramento to plead for restraint. But he refused to
threaten to coerce the state (as Roosevelt had done
in a somewhat similar situation in 1906), and he had
to face a major crisis with Japan. He avoided an open
break by professions of friendship and refusal to rat-

tle the sword, but he did not assuage Japanese public opinion or satisfy the Tokyo government.

It was even more difficult to pursue morality abroad in the one area where really vital American interests were at stake in 1913—Mexico and the Caribbean area. The cornerstone of American foreign policy was the Monroe Doctrine, the integrity of which depended upon naval supremacy in the Caribbean and protection of the Panamanian life line. Wilson and Bryan not only inherited these policies but also believed that the welfare of the entire New World depended upon them. They said, in addition, that they belived in the equality of states and the right of every people to work out their own destiny. They even went so far as to propose, unsuccessfully, a Pan-American Pact guaranteeing the integrity and inviolable sovereignty of the nations of the Western Hemisphere. But how could American interests be protected without recourse to "dollar diplomacy," military intervention, and, if necessary, establishment of protectorates? The answer, Wilson and Bryan thought, lay in moral suasion and helpfulness—in using diplomatic power in the form of recognition, to encourage constitutional stability, and personal intervention, to teach the Mexican and Caribbean peoples how to elect good rulers and govern themselves wisely.

It was easier said than done, especially when the practitioners were somewhat naïve apprentices in diplomacy and lacked wise counselors and diplomatic

agents, in part because Wilson had permitted Bryan
to dismiss the entire professional ministerial corps in
Latin America in order to make room for "deserving
Democrats." Helpfulness in Nicaragua soon turned
into support of a reactionary regime—in other words,
continuation of the policy of the Taft Administration—because Bryan could find no other way to preserve American influence in that country. The desire
to avert anarchy in Haiti after numerous civil wars
led to military occupation of that country. Efforts to
teach constitutional government to the people of the
Dominican Republic led Wilson and Bryan into a
quagmire, the only escape from which was military
intervention, in 1916.

In the beginning it was the same in Mexico, which
was racked by civil war set off in early 1913 when a
military usurper, Victoriano Huerta, overthrew a
constitutional government and seized power as provisional President. Wilson refused to recognize
Huerta, mainly out of revulsion at his bloody methods. He then tried to persuade Huerta and his opponents, the Constitutionalists, to accept his mediation
for establishment of a new constitutional government. Both sides refused, and Huerta hurled flagrant
defiance by establishing a military dictatorship.
Wilson replied by denouncing the Huerta regime
and vowing to destroy it. But Huerta grew stronger,
and Wilson finally had to resort to military force,
sending marines on a flimsy pretext to occupy Vera-
cruz, Huerta's chief port, on April 21, 1914. At the
same time he averted general war by refusing to

expand military operations and by accepting Argen-
tina, Brazil, and Chile's offer of mediation. Wilson
broke Huerta's power and assisted the triumph of the
Constitutionalists in the summer of 1914, but neither
his interference nor his troubles in Mexico were at
an end.

Chapter Five

THE ROAD TO WAR

Woodrow Wilson's apprenticeship, in both national leadership and diplomacy, was over by the summer of 1914. It was well that he had learned quickly, for direr personal and political crises than he had ever known impended, to test his fortitude and wisdom. They seemed to break all at once during that dreadful summer. Wilson's appointment of two conservatives to the new Federal Reserve Board set off a furious reaction from progressives on Capitol Hill and ended in near humiliation of the President. A strike by coal miners in Colorado had just culminated in a bloody civil war and now demanded presidential intervention. In Europe tensions finally burst into general war when Austria-Hungary's determination to punish Serbia for complicity in the murder of the heir to the Austrian and Hungarian thrones set the European alliance machinery into motion. By early August Austria-Hungary and her ally Germany—the so-called Central Powers—were at war with the Entente powers of Russia, France, and Great Britain.

The very foundations of the international community were crumbling, and Wilson could find no solace by turning to his wife, upon whom he had always depended for moral and emotional strength in time of need. She died of tuberculosis of the kidneys and Bright's disease on August 6. Wilson was numb with pain. He grieved so deeply during the following months that he virtually lost the will to live. He was sustained only by the love of family and friends, and he found salvation only in unrelenting work. "It seems, indeed," he wrote, "as if my individual life were blotted out, or, rather, swallowed up, and consisted only of news upon which action must be taken. . . . The day's work must be done, and he must play his full part in doing it. It matters little how much life is left in him when the day is over."

There was much to do, for confusion reigned momentarily at home when the diplomatic powder keg exploded in Europe. There was disorganization of the security markets and financial panic in New York, to be met and overcome by co-operation between the Treasury Department and bankers.

Foreign commerce was in disarray, and Congress responded to Wilson's appeals for measures to stimulate the growth of the American merchant marine. The severest crisis hit the South, because of the collapse of foreign cotton markets. Wilson and the Agriculture and Treasury departments did what they could within conventional limits of federal action, but they stoutly rejected Southern pleas for outright support of cotton prices.

There were, besides, all the urgent tasks attendant upon establishing American neutrality and enforcing policies that would give no undue advantage to either side. Wilson, like the majority of Americans, favored the Entente powers in the belief that they were fighting against German militarism and that their victory would pose no threat to American interests and security. Like a preponderant majority of Americans, Wilson also believed that the United States had no vital stakes in the outcome of the war to justify gratuitous risks of involvement. He therefore proclaimed neutrality in name, and with the help of the State Department set about to establish it in practice. In addition, he took the unusual step, on August 18, of appealing to the American people to curb their predilections and be "impartial in thought as well as in action."

Neutrality in that day did not mean following personal inclination or caprice. It meant accepting duties as well as claiming privileges, and observance of a body of international practices and laws that had been built up over the centuries. A neutral nation, for example, was ordinarily (that is, unless some larger national purposes demanded action otherwise) obliged to sell food and materials, even munitions, to all comers. Throughout the period of American neutrality Wilson resisted the movement fostered by German sympathizers to persuade Congress to impose an embargo on export of munitions. A neutral nation was, moreover, bound to respect the right of belligerents to prevent the flow of contraband (war materials of various categories) by land or sea to enemy territory. Wilson never basically challenged this belligerent right, but as we will see, he made strenuous efforts to keep the channels of peaceful neutral commerce open. A neutral nation could not ordinarily forbid its citizens to lend money to belligerents, any more than it could prevent them from selling goods that money could buy. Wilson permitted Secretary Bryan to impose a moral ban on public loans, in the name of "the true spirit of neutrality," during the first hectic weeks of the war. Both Bryan and Wilson soon recognized that such a policy was discriminatory, in addition to being harmful to American economic interests. Bryan lifted the ban in fact in the spring of 1915; his successor, Robert Lansing, lifted it officially in the following summer. Finally, a neutral government was especially obliged to see that belligerents did not use its territories and port facilities for purposes of war. No one could have been more scrupulous in honoring this obligation than Wilson and his subordinates were.

Great Britain was mistress of the seas in 1914, and

the major task facing Wilson and his advisers in the summer and autumn of that year was coming to an understanding that would protect American neutral trade (that is, commerce in products of no great war value) without denying to Britain the legitimate advantages of dominant sea power. Wilson, at the suggestion of Counselor Robert Lansing of the State Department, proposed that the belligerents all adopt the Declaration of London as their code of maritime warfare. The Declaration, drafted by an international conference in 1908–09, put severe limitations on belligerent sea power, but it had never been ratified and was not part of international law. The British quite understandably objected to its very long free list (articles that could not be prevented from entering enemy territory) and its negation of the old doctrine of continuous voyage (that is, that contraband going to a *neutral* port might be seized if its ultimate destination was enemy territory). Wilson applied heavy personal pressure, but the British refused to put an unamended Declaration of London into effect. He had no recourse but to accept the decision, while warning that the American government would insist upon all rights that its citizens could claim under existing law and treaties.

An acceptable arrangement was worked out because there was basic good will on both sides. The British imposed a far-flung blockade that prevented raw materials susceptible of war usage as well as obvious contraband from going to the Central Powers even through neutral ports. But the British, ever mindful of their dependence on American credit, supplies, and diplomatic good will, were careful, at least in the beginning, to avoid flagrant offense to the American government. They paid for suspected cargoes even when they seized them. They permitted cotton to go to Germany in order to avoid arousing the South, even though they had good grounds for declaring cotton absolute contraband. Wilson and his government could only acquiesce in British measures. The State Department did send a protest to London on December 26, 1914, but it challenged the methods, not the basic legality, of the British maritime system at that time.

Observing a fairly impartial neutrality would have been relatively simple from this point on had the belligerents conducted their warfare within a more or less conventional framework. American business and commerce would have gradually adjusted to the new necessities with few untoward incidents, as they did on the whole in any event. There seemed to be scarcely any possibility of conflict with Germany. Relations were certainly not cordial between the two countries. The great mass of Germans bitterly resented the export of American munitions to their enemies. Many Americans had been outraged by Germany's violation of Belgium's neutrality and condemned what the Allies said were inhuman German methods of warfare. But there could have been no point of dangerous conflict so long as the German government continued to fight only on land.

Wilson and Congress gave convincing testimony,

during the short session that sat between December
1914 and March 1915, to the general American feeling of immunized security. In spite of European dis-
tractions, Congress had time for a major piece of
domestic legislation, a seamen's bill sponsored by
Senator Robert M. La Follette of Wisconsin, to free
seamen from bondage to their labor contracts. It also
considered and nearly adopted a bill establishing a
federal rural credits system. Wilson signed the former and blocked the latter. Wilson and Congress together rather contemptuously rejected the growing
public demand for a rapid increase in the armed
forces. "We are at peace with all the world," Wilson
said in his second Annual Message in December
1914. "No one who speaks counsel based on fact or
drawn from a just and candid interpretation of real-
ities can say that there is reason to fear that from any
quarter our independence or the integrity of our
territory is threatened." Wilson, himself, spent most
of his time and energy during the short session trying
(unsuccessfully, as it turned out) to force through
Congress a bill to create a federally owned and operated merchant fleet.

The whole character of the war at sea was changed,
and Wilson's difficulties were suddenly multiplied,
by the German decision, announced on February 4,
1915, to launch a ruthless submarine war against
Allied merchant shipping in a war zone around the
British Isles. Even neutral ships might be destroyed,
the Germans warned, because it was not always possible to distinguish between neutral and belligerent

merchantmen. The British and French, using the German submarine decree as a pretext, announced on March 1 that they would retaliate by henceforth preventing *all* trade to and from the Central Powers, even commerce in innocent goods through neutral ports. "Both sides," Wilson wrote despairingly, "are seeing red on the other side of the sea, and neutral rights are left, for the time being, out of their reckoning altogether. They listen to necessity (and to necessity as they interpret it), not to reason, and there is therefore no way of calculating or preparing for anything."

Something, none the less, had to be done, lest worse infractions of neutral rights drive the American people to such anger that neutrality would be impossible to maintain. To the British, Wilson sent a sharp protest against misuse of the American flag by British ships and a suggestion that they agree to permit food and raw materials to go to Germany in return for abandonment of the submarine campaign. To the Germans, he dispatched a note on February 10, 1915, warning that the United States would hold the Berlin government to "a strict accountability" for illegal destruction of American lives and ships in the war zone.

It seemed for a time that no crisis would occur. The British, rejecting Wilson's suggestion of an Anglo-German agreement, proceeded to institute a total blockade of Germany, and Wilson seemed to acquiesce. The German naval authorities launched their submarine campaign on February 20, but under

strict orders to respect American shipping. Then a
submarine sank a small British liner, *Falaba,* on
March 28, causing the death, among others, of one
American citizen. The incident provoked a violent
reaction in the American press and set off a spirited
debate within the high Administration circle. Counselor Lansing and other legal advisers argued that the
destruction of the *Falaba* was a flagrant violation of
international morality, and that the American government should assert and defend the right of American citizens to travel on belligerent ships in the war
zone without fear of sudden death. Bryan replied
even more passionately that it was wrong and foolish
to run the risk of war merely to defend a technical
right. Both sides, he went on, were violating international law. The United States had acquiesced in the
British blockade. It should now acquiesce in the
German submarine blockade. It was unfair, Bryan
concluded, to impose a harsher standard on Germany
than on England. Wilson, of course, had to make
what might be the fateful decision. After seeming to
agree with Lansing he veered toward Bryan's view
and decided to send no protest.

Then occurred a catastrophic event that forced Wilson to take some public stand: A German submarine
sank the British liner *Lusitania* in the Irish Sea on
May 7, causing the death of 1,198 persons, among
them being 124 American citizens. To most Americans it was their first introduction to total war against
women and children as well as men, and they recoiled
in indignation and horror. Yet few of the people at

large, and still fewer members of Congress, wanted war. Wilson understood and agreed. "The example of America must be a special example," he said on May 10 in a speech at Philadelphia. "The example of America must be the example not merely of peace because it will not fight, but of peace because peace is the healing and elevating influence of the world and strife is not. There is such a thing as a man being too proud to fight."

He resolved, therefore, to rely upon the spirit rather than the sword, and he appealed in the name of humanity to the German government on May 13 to give up a mode of warfare that was inevitably inhuman. The Germans replied evasively, and Wilson renewed his appeal in more stringent terms on June 9. Bryan, fearing that Wilson's second note carried risks of war, resigned rather than sign it. Wilson named Lansing to his place. The Germans came back more responsively, giving fulsome pledges to respect *American* shipping in the war zone. Wilson returned a third and final *Lusitania* note on July 21 that made German–American understanding possible. It accepted a submarine campaign conducted in "substantial accord" with the rules of cruiser warfare (rules requiring a warship to warn a merchantman and evacuate its crew and passengers to safety before sinking it). Most important, it narrowed the dispute to the single issue of respect for life on *unarmed passenger* liners, while warning that new sinkings of such ships might well lead to hostilities.

Actually, the German Emperor had already sent

top-secret orders to his submarines to spare all *large*
liners. There was, however, still the danger that a
submarine commander might precipitate a new crisis
by an error in judgment or by sinking a small liner.
Such did in fact occur on August 19, when the cap-
tain of the *U-24* sank the British liner *Arabic,* thinking that she was a cargo ship. Wilson now grimly
resolved to have a showdown, even at the risk of a
break in relations. The German government, lacking
enough submarines to offset the disadvantages of
American belligerency, informed Wilson on September 1 that no liners would be sunk without warning
and without provision being made for the safety of
passengers and crew. It was not a final solution—for
the *Lusitania* case still hung fire—but it saved the
precarious peace.

The summer of 1915 was filled with other crises
and alarms for Wilson and a people now distraught
by fear of war. The submarine controversy set off
renewed and more powerful agitation for military
preparedness. Mexico was in virtual chaos as a consequence of civil war within the ranks of the triumphant Constitutionalists. It seemed for a time that
Wilson would have to intervene simply for humani-
tarian reasons. Americans at home were convulsed
by revelations of a far-flung German propaganda organization in the United States. Wilson alone seemed
to keep his head. He endorsed the preparedness
cause, but he made it clear that he, and not fearful
extremists, would define the need. He resisted the
temptation to intervene in Mexico and recognized

the strongest Constitutionalist leader, Venustiano
Carranza. He also found new happiness in the midst
of strife. The pall of grief had lifted when he first
met Edith Bolling Galt in March 1915. Wilson fell
in love almost at once and then pressed a warm and
irresistible campaign to win the lady's hand and
heart. They were married on December 18, 1915.

New perils and unexpected challenges to Wilson's
leadership filled the winter and spring that followed.
The Congress elected in November 1914 met in regular session in December 1915 to hear Wilson present plans for a substantial five-year naval building
program and to increase the regular army, scrap the
state militia, or National Guard, and build an independent reserve force of 400,000 men, to be called
the Continental Army. It was a modest program designed only to provide a modicum of security in the
postwar era. But it provoked such bitter opposition
from progressives, Socialists, and agrarians, especially in the Middle West, that Wilson set out on a
strenuous speaking tour in late January and early
February 1916 to assuage the discontent. He returned
to Washington to find the House Military Affairs
Committee still adamant against the Continental
Army plan and insisting upon retention and strengthening of the National Guard. He had no alternative
but to yield, even though Secretary of War Garrison
resigned in protest, and Wilson's enemies cried
craven surrender.

The gravest peril was the ever-threatening danger
of a break with Germany. The *Arabic* pledge had

brought only momentary assurance, for the German
government was free to begin a campaign of terror
on the seas that might well drive the United States to
war. Difficult negotiations over the *Lusitania* were
in progress by December 1915, with no prospect of
satisfactory settlement. Recent revelations of German
sabotage, plots, and intrigues against American neutrality had alarmed the public and caused Wilson and
his advisers to doubt German professions of friendship. Perhaps the most discouraging aspect of the
situation was the fact that events seemed to have
taken control of foreign policy out of Wilson's hands.

Colonel House thought that he saw a way for Wilson to regain control. The British Foreign Secretary,
Sir Edward Grey, had intimated that the Allies might
accept American mediation and a reasonable peace
if the United States was prepared to give pledges to
join a postwar League of Nations. The chances of
being drawn willy-nilly into the war were, House
knew, already very great. Why not seize the initiative
by coming to agreement with the Allies on terms and
then force the Germans to the peace table? Only if
the Germans refused an armistice or proved un-
reasonable at the peace conference would the United
States have to enter the war. But it would then at
least be fighting for worth-while objectives, not in
defense of dubious maritime rights.

House explained his plan to Wilson at several
meetings between early October and mid-December
of 1915. Wilson was startled at first but grew increasingly enthusiastic. He had hoped and prayed since

the first week of hostilities that he might lead the
warring nations to peace. He had offered his good
offices of mediation, only to have the offer politely
rebuffed. He had sent House on an exploratory
mission to Europe in the early months of 1915, only
to discover that each alliance still thought that it
could impose its will on the other. Perhaps, he
thought, the time was more propitious now. House,
he agreed, should go to London, Paris, and Berlin
to sound out the possibilities of peace on a basis of
disarmament and a postwar League of Nations.
House arrived in London on January 6, 1916, for
conferences with Grey and other members of the
British Cabinet. He then went to Berlin and Paris
for discussions that revealed that neither the German
nor the French government was ready for serious
peace talks. But House thought that the time would
be ripe after the summer campaigns had ended, and
he pressed the British for an understanding after his
return to England in early February. Grey seemed
willing. He and House initialed a memorandum on
February 22 that promised an American call for a
peace conference, in the circumstances explained
above, whenever the *Allies* decided that the time was
opportune.

Actually, neither the French nor the British had
any intention of permitting Wilson's mediation.
House had made it too plain that the American President would be a genuinely neutral mediator who
would work for a peace of reconciliation. The Allies,
like Germany, wanted to win and have their way

entirely. They would accept Wilson's mediation only if it were the sole alternative to defeat and a peace imposed by Germany.

Wilson, on the other hand, took the House-Grey Memorandum so seriously that he risked congressional repudiation and a break with Germany in order to pave the way for action under the memorandum's terms. This somewhat startling situation had its origins in Lansing's negotiations with the German government for settlement of the *Lusitania* case. The Germans conceded virtually everything that the Washington government demanded; in addition, they gave generous new guarantees regarding submarine operations in the Mediterranean. Why not, Lansing suggested, press on to final settlement of the entire vexing submarine controversy? The Germans claimed that it was difficult for submarines to observe traditional rules because the Allies were arming merchantmen and ordering them to attack underwater raiders. Then, let the Allies disarm their steamers on condition that German submarine commanders obey the rules of cruiser warfare in attacking them. Lansing, with Wilson's warm approval, made this proposal formally to the Allied governments on January 18, 1916, warning, besides, that the American government was seriously considering excluding armed merchantmen from its ports. The Germans had meanwhile decided to intensify the submarine campaign around the British Isles. Seizing Lansing's proposal as an excuse, the Berlin government announced on February 10 that its submarines would attack all armed merchant ships without warning in the war zone after February 28, 1916.

British reaction to Lansing's suggestion was so violent that Wilson and Lansing thought they had no choice but to retreat as quickly and gracefully as possible. Lansing announced on February 15 that the American government would not insist that merchantmen disarm should the Allies reject his proposed arrangement; nor, he added, would his Government warn its citizens against traveling on ships that were actually defensively armed. He notified the German ambassador two days later that in view of the new submarine policy he could not accept the German note making amends for the *Lusitania*.

This sudden, seeming reversal set off rumors in Congress that Wilson was maneuvering for war and produced a near panic on Capitol Hill. Democratic members of the House Foreign Affairs Committee agreed unanimously to press for prompt action on a resolution, offered by Representative Jeff McLemore of Texas, warning Americans against traveling on armed ships. It was the most defiant challenge that had yet been raised against Wilson's leadership, and he struck back in a letter to Senator William J. Stone of Missouri, Chairman of the Foreign Relations Committee. He would do his utmost to keep the country at peace, Wilson said, but he would not consent to abridgment of American rights under the German threat. He next met congressional leaders in a "sunrise conference" at the White House on February 25 and reiterated his vow to stand firm. Finally, once he was certain of the outcome, he demanded that the House vote on the McLemore resolution. The House tabled the resolution by a large majority on March 7; the Senate meanwhile had defeated a similar resolution introduced by Thomas P. Gore of Oklahoma.

The way was now clear at home, but never was it more difficult to know where to go. Wilson had reversed what was in fact a policy favorable to Germany and returned to a strict if technical neutrality, in order to pave the way for mediation. But how could he be firm toward Germany without being provocative? The fact was that the Germans had already embarked upon a severe intensification of the submarine war, permitting submarine commanders to sink all belligerent ships, armed and unarmed, without warning, in the war zone. Incidents involving American citizens were bound to occur.

On the American side the first necessity was to redefine policy toward armed merchant ships visiting American ports. Lansing did this in a statement on March 25, which affirmed that merchantmen had a right to carry defensive armament; but the Secretary of State made it clear in subsequent warnings to Allied ambassadors that the American government would permit no armament that gave merchant ships actual fighting equality with submarines.

The second necessity, that of confronting the threat of an intensified U-boat campaign, arose when a German submarine torpedoed the French Channel steamer *Sussex* without warning on March 24, with some eighty casualties. It climaxed a number of incidents, and Wilson resolved to force a final show-down. He sent an ultimatum to Berlin warning that the American government would break diplomatic relations if the Germans did not abandon ruthless methods and give pledges to observe the rules of cruiser warfare in attacking both passenger liners and merchant ships. Wilson made German acceptance possible by omitting any reference in the note to *armed* ships. The Germans yielded on May 4, after many stormy conferences between civilian and military leaders. Their concession, known as the *Sussex* pledge, satisfied Wilson's minimum demand; but it did not extend to armed ships, and it was conditioned upon Wilson's success in forcing the British to observe international law in their own maritime warfare.

Wilson had deliberately if agonizingly run the risk of war, certainly in part because he thought that firmness in the armed ship and *Sussex* crises would help to convince the Allies that he meant to honor every provision of the House-Grey Memorandum. He gave final proof of this intention in a speech before the League to Enforce Peace, in Washington on May 27. The United States, he said, was prepared to abandon its historic isolation and join a postwar League of Nations to prevent aggression and war. Now he turned again, as he had done several times recently, to the British, urging them to consent to mediation on the basis of the House-Grey understanding. The Allies were growing too confident of military victory to run the risks of Wilsonian mediation at a time when the Germans still occupied much of Europe. Grey finally made it unmistakably plain that the Allies would not welcome any peace overtures from Washington. It was a shattering blow to the man who had risked so much in order to make Anglo-American co-operation possible.

No sooner had the *Sussex* crisis ended than the threat of full-scale war with Mexico challenged Wilson's skill and wisdom. It will be recalled that he had tried to cut the Mexican knot in October 1915 by recognizing the Constitutionalist leader, Carranza. This enraged Carranza's chief opponent, Pancho Villa, who maintained a rival regime in northern Mexico. Villa, after murdering American citizens in January in order to provoke military retaliation, raided and burned Columbus, New Mexico, on March 9, 1916, killing nineteen Americans. Public reaction left Wilson no choice but to act. He swiftly assembled military units in Texas and sent a column of 5,000 men, in a "Punitive Expedition" under General John J. Pershing, across the border in pursuit of Villa on March 15. Villa, a superb guerrilla tactician, drew Pershing deeper and deeper into Mexico. The Punitive Expedition had penetrated more than 300 miles by early April, with no prospect of accomplishing its mission.

The Mexican government had meanwhile strongly protested against this violation of its territory. Its discontent, and the anger of the Mexican people, increased the further Pershing went. Then a clash between American and regular Mexican soldiers at

Parral on April 12 led to bloodshed, and Carranza demanded withdrawal of the Punitive Expedition in terms that clearly threatened war. Wilson rejected the demand and mustered out 100,000 troops of the National Guard for service on the border. A second engagement between Mexican and American troops, at Carrizal on June 21, set the war machinery of both governments in motion, and Wilson prepared a war message to deliver to Congress. Then reports revealed that Americans had been the aggressors at Carrizal, and Wilson, suddenly halting what had seemed to be an inexorable movement toward hostilities, eagerly accepted Carranza's suggestion of a joint high commission to negotiate. The commission met between September 6, 1916, and January 15, 1917. It could not reach any accord that Carranza would approve, but it did at least provide an alternative to fighting, and Wilson quietly withdrew the Punitive Expedition on January 27, 1917.

Politicians were making preparations for the impending presidential campaign at the very moment that the nation was struggling through the *Sussex* and Mexican crises to peaceful settlements. Most leaders worked in immense confusion, not knowing the temper of the people or what the issues would be. Republicans were divided almost as badly as they had been in 1912. Eastern conservatives, led by Elihu Root of New York and Senator Henry Cabot Lodge of Massachusetts, were loudly demanding vast preparedness and more firmness toward Germany and Mexico, and Roosevelt was waging a strenuous campaign for the Republican presidential nomination on these issues. The great mass of Republican voters, especially in the Middle West, were, on the other hand, doggedly pacifistic. All congressmen from the Republican states of Iowa, Nebraska, Minnesota, and Wisconsin, for example, voted against tabling the McLemore resolution.

Wilson saw two of the three main facts of American political life as he studied the domestic scene in the early months of 1916. One was that most people wanted only "reasonable," that is, moderate, preparedness. Thus he pushed through a comprehensive program after the *Sussex* crisis that satisfied the vague public desire for security without seeming to be warlike. It provided substantial increases in naval building in a one-year program, doubled the regular army, and vastly increased the National Guard, at the same time putting it more securely under the War Department's control. It also included provisions for a Council of National Defense and a federally owned and operated merchant fleet.

Wilson could not fail to see the more obvious second fact, that he and his party were almost surely bound to lose the Presidency and control of Congress if they did not win a substantial portion of the now-disintegrating Progressive party. Too many people ordinarily voted Republican. It was as plain as daylight to Wilson what he had to do. He had to convince Progressives and independents that the Democratic party had cut loose from State rights moorings and was capable of undertaking bold national reconstruction, even though this meant commitment to nationalistic progressivism such as Roosevelt had championed in 1912. Wilson's decision to yield to political necessity was made easier by his growing conviction that this was in fact the right thing to do.

He began auspiciously early in 1916, by nominating Brandeis to the Supreme Court, and by winning his confirmation in one of the hardest confirmation battles in the history of the United States Senate. Wilson next, in the spring of 1916, pushed through a measure giving near autonomy to the Philippine Islands. At the same time he revived the rural credits bill, which he had twice blocked, and won its adoption in May. These were the first signs of progress toward the New Nationalism.

All observers, Democratic and Republican, saw the third and most important fact of domestic political life clearly enough once the national conventions met in June. It was the passionate desire of the majority in all sections to avoid involvement in the European war. The Republicans responded by rejecting the belligerent Roosevelt and nominating Justice Charles Evans Hughes on a platform demanding only "reasonable" preparedness and a strict neutrality. The Democratic convention, contrary to Wilson's plans and expectations, riotously demonstrated for neutrality and peace. It renominated Wilson by acclamation, Bryan said, because he had kept the country out of war.

Victory, it was obvious at the outset of the campaign, would go to the candidate who could most deftly ride the two great waves of progressivism and peace. Hughes was fatally handicapped. He could not affirm his own progressivism without alienating Republican conservatives; he could not take a clear position on foreign policy without disaffecting either the Eastern champions of strong diplomacy or the Midwestern isolationists and the German-Americans. He had to rely on generalities and captious criticism, and he gave the impression of being wholly ineffective.

This was true above all because Wilson had the leadership of the progressive and peace forces and kept Hughes reeling all through the campaign. He made a bold bid for labor support in averting a nation-wide railroad strike in August by winning adoption of the Adamson Act that imposed the eight-hour day for railroad workers. He pleased social justice progressives by forcing adoption of a model workmen's compensation bill for federal employees and of a national child labor bill. He pacified business progressives by exacting a tariff commission and protection for the chemical industry from reluctant Democrats in Congress. He approved when Southern and Western agrarians forced a stiff increase in the income tax and imposed new taxes on munitions makers and estates. Most important, he not only permitted Democratic speakers and propagandists to use the slogan "He kept us out of war" without stint, but he also took up the battle cry of peace himself.

It was a spectacular campaign, but it did not seem enough to convert the normal Democratic minority into a majority when first returns came in on election night, November 7, 1916. Hughes made almost a clean sweep of the East and Middle West, and Wilson went to bed thinking that he had lost. Then returns from the Plains states and the West revealed a strong Wilson tide in those sections, because former Socialists, independents, women voters, and former Progressives had moved en masse into the Democratic column. In the final count Wilson had a majority of twenty-three in the Electoral College and 9,129,606 popular votes to 8,538,221 for Hughes.

To Wilson the chief significance of the election returns was their testimony to the deep popular desire to avoid war in order to maintain so-called neutral rights on the seas. And yet he also knew that the war was entering a new stage, in which both sides would use all weapons at their command to break the deadlock, and that American neutrality might well be impossible in these cruel circumstances. The only certain way to guarantee American security and peace, Wilson knew, was to bring the war to an end.

The Germans, staggering and wondering if they could survive much longer, were eager for Wilson to move quickly. But they wanted Wilson's help only in forcing the Allies to accept an armistice, not his presence at a peace conference. The Allies did not believe that they could permit any peace discussions so long as the Germans held precious hostages in the form of Belgian, French, and Russian territory. But there was also the danger that the Germans might bid for all-out victory through an unlimited submarine campaign if Wilson did nothing. Indeed, the German Chancellor announced on December 12, 1916, that his government was prepared to negotiate; it was his own attempt to forestall ruthless submarine warfare.

In these dangerous circumstances Wilson decided to proceed, in spite of grave warnings from House and Lansing that he might find himself in virtual entente with Germany. He took the first step on December 18, appealing to the belligerents to state their war aims. The Allies responded specifically on January 12, 1917. The Germans refused to divulge peace terms, deciding on January 9 to try to achieve complete victory by a submarine campaign against all shipping, belligerent *and* neutral. They expected American belligerency in consequence, but they were confident that they could win before the United States could mobilize and intervene decisively. Wilson had meanwhile begun direct secret negotiations with the British and German governments, and he went before the Senate on January 22 to deliver what was in fact a clarion call to the entire world. It was a plea for a "peace without victory," for, he said, only a "peace between equals" could endure.

The German government returned two replies on January 31. One encouraged Wilson's peace efforts and divulged German terms for the first time. The other announced that German submarines would sink *all* ships without warning in European waters and the eastern Mediterranean after February 1. The future course of history depended on Wilson's decision. It was to break diplomatic relations with Germany on February 3, *but to do everything possible to avoid open hostilities.* That, as it turned out, was not so easily done. Goods began to pile up on wharves when American and other neutral ships refused to enter the war zones without protection. Then came the sinking without warning of the British liner *Laconia,* with great loss of life, and more important, revelation of a telegram from Arthur Zimmermann, German Foreign Secretary, inviting the Mexicans to sign an alliance, to go into effect only in the event that the United States entered the European war. By its terms Mexico would come into the war against the United States and receive Texas, New Mexico, and Arizona as reward. Wilson was so shocked and angered that he asked Congress for authority to arm American merchantmen. A small group of pacifists in the Senate prevented congressional action before adjournment on March 4, but Wilson found authority under an old statute and took action on March 9.

The United States, as Wilson said in his second Inaugural on March 5, was now committed to armed neutrality and avoidance of full-fledged belligerency. And yet events were transpiring and convictions were forming in Wilson's mind to drive the nation into war relentlessly within a month. Public opinion was highly agitated, and at least a large minority of leaders and newspapers were demanding a declaration of war. Their outcry seemed almost irresistible when German submarines sank three American merchantmen without warning on the same day, March 18.

At this moment of mounting frenzy the first Russian Revolution overthrew the despotic czarist regime, establishing a liberal government. This occurrence ended all doubt for many Americans about whether the Allies were truly fighting for democracy.

The decision, actually, was in Wilson's hands, so divided and distraught were the American people. He decided, apparently on March 19, to accept belligerency. Armed neutrality, his naval advisers had told him, would lead to hostilities in any event. The German submarine campaign, he also knew, was succeeding and, if uncurbed, might end in a vindictive German peace. But what made belligerency acceptable in the showdown in Wilson's agonized mind was the conviction that the war could not last beyond the summer of 1917 if the German bid was thwarted. American intervention would therefore shorten Europe's ordeal, not prolong it. And belligerency would give Wilson what he wanted most passionately—a seat at the peace table, where he could work, with all the power and might of the United States and the strength of his principles behind him, for a peace of reconciliation.

Having made the decision, Wilson called Congress into special session for April 2. He knew the awful risks of leading a great people into war, but there seemed to be no alternative, and he appeared before the lawmakers on the appointed day to ask that they recognize the state of war that already existed by choice of the Imperial German Government. After discussing steps to put the country on a war footing,

Wilson turned abruptly to the large issues and objectives of the war. It was being waged, he said (for the first time), because the Imperial German military autocracy had embarked upon a campaign against liberty everywhere. "The world," he cried, "must be made safe for democracy." The American people would give their blood and treasure for the things they had always carried nearest their hearts—"for democracy, for the right of those who submit to authority to have a voice in their own Governments, for the rights and liberties of small nations, for a universal dominion of right by such a concert of free peoples as shall bring peace and safety to all nations and make the world itself at last free." "To such a task," he concluded, "we can dedicate our lives and our fortunes, everything that we are and everything that we have, with the pride of those who know that the day has come when America is privileged to spend her blood and her might for the principles that gave her birth and happiness and the peace which she has treasured. God helping her, she can do no other."

Chapter Six

GIRDING ON THE SWORD

The Senate approved the war resolution on April 4, 1917, the House on April 6. Wilson signed the document early in the afternoon of April 7, and news of American belligerency was flashed minutes later around the world. Neutrality was over, but no one in the United States truly knew what belligerency would involve. All Americans, Wilson included, had visualized intervention in terms of massive financial and material contributions, participation in the war against the submarines, and dispatch of a small expeditionary force. Events soon revealed the optimism of American calculations. The Allies were in desperate straits. The German submarine campaign was succeeding beyond the expectations of its ardent champions. Worse still, the Allies had begun to scrape the bottom of the manpower barrel and faced a dire "crisis of reserves." Defeat seemed nearer than victory.

Meeting the challenge was of course the entire nation's business, but direction and ultimate decision fell to Wilson. Never before had events come crowding in so relentlessly upon his days. His method in industrial and military mobilization was simply a refinement of customary procedure: to determine the best solutions by common counsel, then to find the best men to achieve them, and to support them to the hilt. Unhappily, solutions were not always easily achieved, even by the best counsel and administrative method. Then new approaches had to be tried. Always there was work, unending work, to be done, and almost no time for healing rest and recuperation.

Military necessities were most immediately obvious and urgent. Adoption of the war resolution found the United States Navy ready and eager to fight, but Wilson had to intervene strenuously, over some nearly dead bodies in the British Admiralty, to enable the American navy to make its decisive contribution—institution of a convoy system that assured the flow of life-giving supplies and men. The army had to start virtually from scratch in what turned out to be literally a race against disaster. The Army War College had made elaborate plans on paper, and

Wilson, using all his powers of persuasion and compulsion, forced a Selective Service bill through Congress in early May 1917, in spite of the bitter opposition of pacifists and Southern and Western agrarians. He also had to thwart the efforts of friends of Theodore Roosevelt to include a provision to compel the army to accept a division that Roosevelt had already recruited. Draft boards in every locality eventually inducted nearly three million men into the army. Volunteer enlistments in all branches of the armed services brought the total number of Americans under arms by the end of the war to 4,800,000. Some 112,000 of them died while in service.

Never in history has a great nation had a more unwarlike commander in chief than Wilson. He was, to be sure, as reliable and orderly in administration of military affairs as of other matters. He stood behind his Secretary of War, Newton D. Baker, in the face of ferocious assaults and accusations of inefficiency. Wilson also supported his commander of the American Expeditionary Force, General Pershing, in Pershing's determination to create and preserve an independent command in France, in spite of Allied demands that American units be amalgamated into French and British commands. Nor did Wilson ever want to stint in sacrifice. Even so, the burden of responsibility lay heavily on his mind and heart. Having been denied the blessing of sons of his own, he took all "his boys" as sons to his heart and admonished them over and over to fight bravely and well, and to stand in the evil day. "The eyes of all the world will be upon you, because you are in some special sense the soldiers of freedom," he counseled soldiers on September 4, 1917, for example. "Let it be your pride, therefore, to show all men everywhere not only what good soldiers you are, but also what good men you are, keeping yourselves fit and straight in everything, and pure and clean through and through." Wilson appointed a former student, Raymond B. Fosdick, to undertake a vast effort for the recreational and spiritual welfare of sailors and soldiers at home and on the fighting fronts.

Such blood, he resolved, must not be shed vainly; such sacrifice could not be tarnished by greed or slothfulness or subversion at home. The whole nation must rally even as its sons were responding to duty's call. Wilson, only a week after adoption of the war resolution, signed an executive order creating a Committee on Public Information to mobilize opinion behind the war effort, and appointed George Creel, a journalist from Denver, to head the new agency. Public sentiment was still divided on the wisdom of participation, and Creel organized what was up to that time probably the most gigantic propaganda effort in history to convert (and coerce) the antiwar minority. He took his main theme from Wilson's war message and subsequent addresses. But Creel also appropriated Allied propaganda that portrayed the alleged German menace in lurid colors, and he encouraged a hatred of everything German and a war hysteria that needed no stimulation to run to awful excess. Wilson tried occasionally to dampen

fanaticism that proscribed German opera or the
teaching of German in public schools. He made it
plain throughout the war that Americans had no
quarrel with the German people and no jealousy of
German culture. But he did not and could not hold
back the tide of hysteria. It was beyond his or any
man's control.

Indeed, Wilson made his own contribution to this
dark chapter by signing two measures that furnished
lethal weapons to suppress dissent. The first, the
Espionage Act of 1917, forbade obstruction of the
draft or aid to the enemy and gave the Postmaster
General rather wide powers of censorship. The second, the Sedition Act of 1918, provided punishment
for any kind of sedition and utterances disrespectful
of the government. The Justice Department was not
gentle in enforcement, particularly against a radical
labor organization, the Industrial Workers of the
World, and Socialists who continued to oppose participation in the war. Eugene V. Debs, Socialist leader,
was brought to trial for opposition to belligerency,
for example, and sentenced to prison for ten years.
Wilson regretted excesses, but he was not inclined
to mercy in civil rights cases. He could never look
a soldier in the face again, he told a friend, if he
pardoned Debs and others like him who had tried
to weaken America's determination to support her
fighting men. Such an attitude was at least under-
standable in a man upon whose decisions the very
safety of the nation depended. Abraham Lincoln and
Franklin D. Roosevelt, both liberals and humani-

tarians, resorted to measures as stern under duress.

All told, the First World War cost the American people some $33,500,000,000 up to 1920, and determining how much of the costs should be borrowed and how much raised by taxes provoked a running fight in Congress all through the period of American belligerency. Conservatives of both parties wanted heavy borrowing and consumption taxes and only moderate increases in the income tax. Progressives, agrarians, and radicals believed that the wealthy classes, who, they thought, had driven the country into war, should be made to bear all the costs. Some of them, like Senator La Follette, wanted to confiscate all incomes over $100,000 a year.

Wilson and Secretary of the Treasury McAdoo threw their support increasingly behind the radicals. The War Revenue Act of 1917, the highest tax measure in American history to that time, imposed, among other things, a graduated excess profits tax and increased the maximum tax on incomes to 67 per cent. Still it was not enough to meet the inexorable demands of a war economy, and Wilson appeared before a joint session of Congress on May 27, 1918, to urge steep increases. "The people of this country are not only united in the resolute purpose to win this war," he said, "but are ready and willing to bear any burden and undergo any sacrifice that it may be necessary for them to bear in order to win it." The Revenue Act of 1918 brought the maximum tax on incomes to 77 per cent and increased the excess profits tax to a maximum of 65 per cent. These measures put democracy to work at home, with considerable vengeance. They imposed from three quarters to four fifths of the tax burden on large incomes, profits, and inheritances, and they caused the wealthy classes—in spite of some cases of swollen profits—to suffer sizable economic losses as a result of the war. They also generated deep bitterness against the Democratic leader, and determination to turn his party out of office at all costs in 1920.

Equally if not more offensive to reactionary manufacturers and businessmen was the Wilson Administration's determination to protect labor's rights and enhance its welfare even during wartime. This, Wilson said, was labor's war. He did not hesitate to move against violence or strikes that imperiled the war effort. But through agencies in the War and Navy departments and the National War Labor Board and War Labor Policies Board, he set the entire federal power behind organized labor's demand for recognition, the eight-hour day when possible, and wage increases to offset rising costs of living. In addition, he obtained a new federal child labor law when in 1918 the Supreme Court declared the Child Labor Act of 1916 unconstitutional. Two results of Wilson's massive intervention on labor's behalf were particularly striking. Membership in the American Federation of Labor increased from 2,072,702 in 1916, to 3,260,168 in 1918. And labor's *real* income increased 20 per cent between 1916 and 1918, in spite of a sharp decline in the hours of labor and the widespread institution of the eight-hour day.

Wilson's main task at home was of course to guide the vast and complicated industrial and agricultural economies and railroad system into a mobilization that would yield food for the Allies and an unending stream of supplies to the Allied and burgeoning American armies. No American experiences in the past furnished precedents for guide lines, while the very idea of intimate governmental direction and control was repugnant to most businessmen. It was little wonder that the machinery of industrial mobilization creaked and proved inefficient until it could be perfected, and failed outright in several instances.

Wilson began slowly and experimentally, relying in the beginning on voluntary efforts and his own inherent war powers when he could, without resort to coercive legislation. He appointed Herbert Hoover, former director of the Belgian Relief Commission, as head of a voluntary food control program to stimulate agricultural production and curb domestic consumption. Soon, however, Wilson had to ask for and receive, in the Lever Act of August 1917, sweeping authority over production, manufacture, and distribution of foodstuffs, fuel, fertilizers, and farm implements. He appointed Hoover head of a Food Administration and Harry A. Garfield, president of Williams College, head of a Fuel Administration, both with extraordinary powers. Garfield kept war factories running in spite of coal shortages and several transportation crises. Hoover was even more successful, increasing the export of foodstuffs from a prewar average of some 7,000,000 tons, to 12,327,000 tons

in 1917–18, and to 18,667,000 in 1918–19. Keeping
the railroads running under the weight of wartime
traffic was another indispensable task. Wilson relied
at first on a voluntary Railroads War Board for direction. But when it failed to avert what seemed to
be a spreading paralysis, Wilson did not hesitate to
take control. He established a United States Railroad
Administration on December 28, 1917, and put Mc-
Adoo in command.

The main problem in industrial mobilization was
devising some system to assure a plentiful flow of
scarce raw materials to munitions factories, shipyards,
and the like. Inherent difficulties were compounded
by the fact that adoption of the war resolution found
American industry and labor already working to the
limit, so that an increase in one branch of industry
meant inevitably a decrease in another. A Munitions
Standards Board, created by the Council of National
Defense on March 31, 1917, failed to establish authority over the American armed services and Allied
purchasing agencies. The Council of National Defense abolished the Munitions Standards Board on
July 28 and substituted a War Industries Board, to
control production, allocate scarce raw materials,
and supervise labor relations. This latter board made
some progress but failed to establish sufficient control
over the War and Navy departments and steel manufacturers. It seemed by the end of 1917 that the war
effort at home was either collapsing or in chaos. Much
of the difficulty was due to an extraordinarily severe
winter, which momentarily crippled the railroads,

but an investigation by the Senate Military Affairs
Committee revealed that soldiers in training camps
had not been provided adequate shelter and clothing.
"The Military Establishment of America has fallen
down," exclaimed the chairman of the Committee on
January 19, 1918. ". . . It has almost stopped functioning . . . because of inefficiency in every bureau and in
every department of the Government." Conservative
Republicans now mounted a tremendous campaign
aimed at nothing less than establishment of a coalition War Cabinet to take control of the war effort
out of the President's hands.

It was one of the sharpest crises in Wilson's career
as domestic leader. He knew what fundamental issue
was at stake, for he had seen English Conservatives
exploit similar circumstances and use similar tactics
to destroy a Liberal government and seize power in
London under the guise of Coalition. He was also
furious. "Called upon W. W. and found him in a
fighting mood. His jaw was set. His eyes shot fire,"
Senator Henry F. Ashurst of Arizona wrote in his
diary on January 22, 1918. Wilson struck back au-
daciously by writing out a measure, which became
the Overman Act, conferring on *himself* almost dic-
tatorial power to organize and direct the nation's
resources. Congress approved the bill in May. Wilson,
however, had meanwhile, on March 6, appointed
Bernard M. Baruch, a Wall Street broker, as chairman
of the War Industries Board and conferred sweeping
powers over priorities and production on the re-
organized agency.

Wilson and Baruch worked in perfect harmony. Wilson liked and trusted Baruch, but he did not fail to give careful personal direction to his subordinate. Baruch for his part had a genius for organization and enough ruthlessness to dragoon big businessmen. He straightway harnessed the gigantic American industrial machine and brought such order into the mobilization effort that criticism subsided to a partisan murmur.

There were, inevitably, failures as well as triumphs. American ordnance factories were not prepared to produce heavy guns and tanks in quantity until the end of the war. An Aircraft Production Board made several bad starts before aircraft production got into high gear. A vast shipbuilding program faltered under inefficient leadership, and fulfilled expectations only during the last months of the war. Yet the remarkable thing was that so much was done in so little time. There were more than half a million American soldiers in France by May 1918; their number had grown to 1,200,000 by early September. Plans called for an American force in France of between two and three million men for a final great offensive in the spring of 1919. American industry and shipping would have been prepared and able to supply this force. Not a little of the credit for this accomplishment belonged to Wilson for his faith and patience and his careful attention to day-to-day details. No important decision was made without his knowledge and consent. His mind was the nerve center of the whole American war effort.

It would all be vain, indeed unbelievably wicked, Wilson believed, if such power as the Allies and the United States were mounting on the western front were used for the wrong ends. But who would determine what ends were "right" and what were "wrong"? Wilson believed that great, almost apocalyptic, forces were locked in combat in the war. In his mind the chief combatants were German military autocracy and western parliamentary democracy. But he also believed that the conflict was in part a civil war. On the one side stood parties and groups who represented the rising tide of liberal humanitarianism—liberals, labor leaders, social and economic reformers, and the like, in Germany and Austria-Hungary as well as in the Allied nations and the United States. Against them stood the forces of reaction, militarism, and imperialism, whose chief spokesmen were leaders in big business and international finance. They dominated the Republican party in the United States and the Coalition government of Prime Minister David Lloyd George in Great Britain, Wilson thought, almost as much as the Kaiser's government in Berlin.

American war aims, Wilson knew, were not necessarily Allied war aims. The United States had entered the war asking and expecting nothing except a new world community based on justice and organized to prevent future wars. The Allies wanted and had made arrangements for other things as well. Wilson knew the Allied terms as they had been announced even before he made his own decision to accept belligerency. He knew about some of the secret Allied understandings, most certainly those concerning Italy and probably those concerning Japan, within two months after adoption of the war resolution. He might have forced the Allies to an understanding on peace terms as the price of American intervention; indeed, many Allied diplomats expected him to do so. Instead, having already announced American objectives generally in his "Peace without Victory" speech, he postponed the day of reckoning, confident that he could force the Allies to his way of thinking at the end of the war because by that time they would be financially in his hands.

Meanwhile, Wilson made it clear that the United States was fighting as an Associate and not an Allied power. This posture emphasized what was in fact true, that the United States had no commitment to Allied understandings. More important, it freed Wilson to stand with increasing boldness as spokesman, not merely of the American people, but also of men everywhere who wanted peace based on principles instead of privileges and plunder. Various groups of pacifists, idealists, and labor intellectuals had already worked out what might be called a liberal international program well before the United States entered the war. It called for open diplomacy, democratically controlled; self-determination for subject peoples; disarmament; no indemnities or annexations; and, above all, a postwar international organization to preserve peace. Wilson took moral leadership of the movement in his address before the League to Enforce Peace, on May 27, 1916, and in his "Peace without Victory" speech of January 22, 1917. Between these two utterances he also established contact with leaders of the liberal peace movement in Great Britain.

It was all the more important, Wilson thought, to encourage and speak for this surging and irresistible movement now that the United States was in the war. It was important that the world know that Americans were fighting for a peace of justice and reconciliation. But it was not so easy for Wilson to speak out now that he was a belligerent. From every quarter—from Washington as well as Paris and London—came warnings that peace talk might divide the Allies and was, moreover, dangerous so long as the Germans occupied Allied territory. The adoption, by the Russian government and the German *Reichstag* (parliament) in the midsummer of 1917, of resolutions calling for a peace based on the principles of no annexations and no indemnities stirred Wilson mightily, as did a peace appeal by Pope Benedict XV on August 1, 1917. Wilson was strongly tempted to reply with a definitive statement of war aims but held back out of fear of "dissenting voices from France or Italy." But he asked Colonel House to assemble a group of experts, subsequently known as The Inquiry, to formulate specific objectives. He also sent House to London in October, in part to press the British and French for agreement on war aims.

The opportunity, indeed the utter necessity, came almost as soon as House arrived in London. The

Bolsheviks (radical Russian Socialists) overthrew the
moderate Socialist government of Russia on November 7, 1917, and appealed at once to Russia's western
allies to begin peace negotiations on a basis of no
annexations and no indemnities. Wilson was eager to
respond, but Allied leaders refused to issue even an
innocuous general statement. Then the Bolsheviks
concluded an armistice with Germany, published Russia's secret treaties for the division of war spoils,
and called upon workers in all belligerent countries
to overthrow their allegedly avaricious and imperialistic rulers. In addition, the Austrian Foreign Minister declared on Christmas Day that the Central
Powers desired no forcible annexations. Something
had to be said. Liberals, Socialists, and labor leaders
in the United States and Great Britain—the very
groups upon whom Wilson relied for mass support
—were demanding a forthright avowal. Delay would
only give credence to Bolshevik accusations.

Without consulting leaders in London and Paris
—that would be futile and stultifying, anyway, Wilson thought—Wilson set to work with Colonel House
on January 4 and 5, 1918. Using a long memorandum
prepared by "The Inquiry" as a guide, Wilson hammered out an address intended to make American
peace objectives so clear that neither Bolsheviks nor
Allied statesmen could fail to understand. Then he
went before a joint session of Congress on January 8
to deliver what was at once called the Fourteen Points
address. He began by saying that it was evident that
the military masters of Germany were determined

to subjugate the helpless Russian people, and that
the time had come for peace-loving nations to avow
the objectives for which they were fighting. These
Wilson proceeded to enumerate in general and
specific points. The former called for open diplomacy,
freedom of the seas ("except as the seas may be closed
in whole or in part by international action for the
enforcement of international covenants"), general
disarmament, removal of barriers to international
trade, an impartial settlement of colonial claims, and
establishment of a League of Nations "affording mutual guarantees of political independence and territorial integrity to great and small states alike." Two
of the specific points—restoration of Belgium and
self-determination for the Russian people—were, Wilson said, indispensable. Others not quite so vital
included the return of Alsace-Lorraine to France, establishment of an independent Poland, autonomy for
the subject peoples of Austria-Hungary, and satisfaction of Italy's legitimate claims to the Italian-speaking
parts of Austria. Finally, there was an appeal to the
German people, promising them acceptance and "a
place of equality" in the postwar international community, and a moving peroration:

> We have spoken now, surely, in terms too concrete
> to admit of any further doubt or question. An evi-
> dent principle runs through the whole program I
> have outlined. It is the principle of justice to all
> peoples and nationalities, and their right to live on
> equal terms of liberty and safety with one another,
> whether they be strong or weak. Unless this principle

be made its foundation no part of the structure of international justice can stand. The people of the United States could act upon no other principle; and to the vindication of this principle they are ready to devote their lives, their honor, and everything that they possess. The moral climax of this the culminating and final war for human liberty has come, and they are ready to put their own strength, their own highest purpose, their own integrity and devotion to the test.

The Fourteen Points address was western democracy's answer to the Bolshevik appeal for destruction of the old world in the fire of class warfare and creation of a new world-wide dictatorship of the so-called proletariat. The Fourteen Points so skillfully combined what might be called legitimate Allied peace aims with the liberal peace program that it immediately became the great, single manifesto of the war —the standard to which all liberals, many Germans included, could rally.

It seemed for a moment that the Austrians and Germans might respond seriously to begin peace talks. Wilson came back eagerly to Congress to report on progress on February 11. Peace conversations, he said, depended upon whether the belligerents could agree upon what were later called Four Supplementary Points:

> First, that each part of the final settlement must be based upon the essential justice of that particular case and upon such adjustments as are most likely to bring a peace that will be permanent;
>
> Second, that peoples and provinces are not to be

bartered about from sovereignty to sovereignty as if
they were mere chattels and pawns in a game, even
the great game, now forever discredited, of the balance of power; but that

Third, every territorial settlement involved in this
war must be made in the interest and for the benefit
of the populations concerned, and not as a part of
any mere adjustment or compromise of claims
amongst rival states; and

Fourth, that all well-defined national aspiration
shall be accorded the utmost satisfaction that can be
accorded them without introducing new or perpetu-
ating old elements of discord and antagonism that
would be likely in time to break the peace of Europe
and consequently of the world.

Then the Germans shattered Wilson's hopes for
a negotiated settlement. First, they imposed a Car-
thaginian peace treaty on the Bolsheviks at Brest-
Litovsk on March 3. Second, they launched a great
offensive on the western front to knock France out
of the war before large American reinforcements
could arrive. There was no choice, Wilson cried on
April 6, but "Force, Force to the utmost, Force
without stint or limit, the righteous and triumphant
Force which shall make Right the law of the world,
and cast every selfish dominion down in the dust."

The German drive, known as the second Marne
offensive, came perilously close to succeeding, and
intensified military problems that had long plagued
Wilson and his advisers. In the long run, however,
it had a more significant political than military impact, for the menace of a German victory drove Allied

and American leaders to new policies and decisions
that helped to change the course of history.

One of these was a change in policy toward Austria-
Hungary. Wilson and the Allied leaders had long
said that Europe's peace could never be secure without some satisfaction of the nationalistic aspirations
of the subject peoples of the Hapsburg Empire. But
no responsible western leader before 1918 wanted
to destroy the dynasty or the unity that it had imposed on south central Europe. The Allied and
American objective was *federalization* of the Empire,
and Wilson conducted secret negotiations all through
1917 and early 1918 to persuade leaders in Vienna
to make a separate peace on a basis of imperial
reorganization. These efforts foundered upon the
opposition of the Magyar rulers of Hungary. Meanwhile, Czech leaders in exile were pressing in London
and Washington for recognition of the claims of their
people to *independence,* achievement of which could
only mean destruction of the Empire. The Czechs had
more than the principle of self-determination on their
side. They also had a sizable army in Russia, called
the Czech Legion—composed of former prisoners of
war—to offer in return for recognition. The lure was
too attractive for the hard-pressed Allied leaders. The
British recognized the Czechoslovak National Council as the provisional government of the new nation
on August 9. There was nothing that Wilson could do
but follow suit on September 3. He knew that the
Austro-Hungarian Empire was crumbling in any
event.

The threat of German victory produced a more spectacular if no more important convulsion in Allied and American policy toward Russia. Western leaders continued to hope, between the signing of the Russo-German armistice in December 1917 and the Treaty of Brest-Litovsk in March 1918, that the Russians would somehow maintain an effort on the eastern front. The Bolshevik surrender at Brest-Litovsk and the subsequent German second Marne offensive caused British and French military leaders to make wild and frenzied plans to re-establish the eastern front through intervention to support anti-Bolshevik factions and the Czech Legion in Russia. The British and French governments, joined by Colonel House, Secretary Lansing, and the Japanese government (which had certain designs on Siberia), applied heavy pressure on Wilson all through the spring and early summer of 1918 to approve various projects of intervention. He did not believe that they were either practical or right in principle. But the pressure became too great to be resisted entirely, and Wilson, after "sweating blood," yielded on August 3. He agreed to join the British in sending a small force to Archangel and Murmansk, in northern Russian, to protect military supplies from seizure by the Germans. He also consented to join the Japanese in sending a small expedition to Vladivostok, in Siberia, mainly to guarantee a safe exit for the Czech Legion, which was now fighting the Bolsheviks, in part to keep a close eye on Japanese activities and intrigues.

The main results of these so-called interventions,

as well as of other similar British and French efforts elsewhere, was to strengthen the Bolsheviks and give some credence to their charges that the imperialistic western powers were trying to strangle the Soviet state in its infancy. It was supremely ironic when Soviet historians in the 1950's turned their condemnation against Wilson, accusing him of being the chief author of the capitalistic plot.

Meanwhile, Wilson's hardest and most vital task after March 1918 was to dam the tide of war lust, intensified by the second Marne offensive, which threatened to engulf the American people even as it had already swept over the peoples of Europe. There was the danger that he and his people would succumb to the fascinations of total war, become intoxicated with hatred of the enemy and love of fighting, and forget the great political objectives which they had taken up the sword to vindicate.

Wilson more than any other major belligerent leader kept a clear head and uncorrupted heart. Never once, insofar as we know, did he lust for victory and vengeance. Never once was he not eager to stop the fighting as soon as political objectives had been attained. His answer to the German thrust to the Marne was not only "Force without stint or limit," but also to renew his moral offensive for a righteous peace.

He began with an address at Mount Vernon on July 4, 1918. "The Past and the Present are in deadly grapple and the peoples of the world are being done to death between them," he cried. There could be no compromise of basic principles. "These," he went on, "are the ends for which the associated peoples of the world are fighting and which must be conceded them before there can be peace:

I. The destruction of every arbitrary power anywhere that can separately, secretly, and of its single choice disturb the peace of the world; or, if it cannot be presently destroyed, at the least its reduction to virtual impotence.

II. The settlement of every question, whether of territory, of sovereignty, of economic arrangement, or of political relationship, upon the basis of the free acceptance of that settlement by the people immediately concerned, and not upon the basis of the material interest or advantage of any other nation or people which may desire a different settlement for the sake of its own exterior influence or mastery.

III. The consent of all nations to be governed in their conduct towards each other by the same principles of honor and of respect for the common law of civilized society that govern the individual citizens of all modern states in their relations with one another; to the end that all promises and covenants may be sacredly observed, no private plots or conspiracies hatched, no selfish injuries wrought with impunity, and a mutual trust established upon the handsome foundation of a mutual respect for right.

IV. The establishment of an organization of peace which shall make it certain that the combined power of free nations will check every invasion of right and serve to make peace and justice the more secure by affording a definite tribunal of opinion to which all must submit and by which every international readjustment that cannot be amicably agreed upon by the peoples directly concerned shall be sanctioned.

Wilson's climax came with his so-called Five Additional Points, enunciated in a speech in New York opening the fourth Liberty Loan campaign on September 27. They recapitulated much of what he had said since the Fourteen Points, but they also gave greater emphasis to the need for a future League of Nations.

Chapter Seven

THE HOPE OF MANKIND

Allied and American armies were making war with
increasing fury while Wilson prepared for peace. The
German assault was spent by mid-July of 1918, and
the Allies with growing American support began a
counteroffensive that was thrusting to the German
frontier by early October. The panic-stricken Germans appealed to Wilson on October 3 for an armistice, looking toward a settlement based on Wilson's
Fourteen Points and subsequent addresses. Actually,
the German military leaders hoped to obtain a res-
pite to prepare new defenses. Wilson negotiated
with consummate skill, making it clear that he

137

would accept no arrangement that gave the Germans any opportunity to resume hostilities. He also made it plain that he and the Allies would deal only with a responsible civilian government, not with the German military autocracy. The German will to fight collapsed so rapidly under the impact of these negotiations that the civilian leaders were able to take control and agree to all of Wilson's demands on October 23.

Wilson now sent Colonel House to Paris to force a showdown with the Allied prime ministers and generals. There was a stormy conference on October 29, and House used the dark threat of a separate American peace on the following day to head off a host of objections. The result was retreat to mutually acceptable common ground. The Allied leaders approved the Fourteen Points in principle; Wilson in turn accepted a British reservation of freedom of action on Point Two, concerning freedom of the seas, and a stipulation that the Germans should be told that they would be compelled to make reparation for all civilian damages caused by their aggression. Allied generals prepared military terms while the political leaders debated, and German representatives signed the combined military and political articles, known as the Pre-Armistice Agreement, on November 11. It was tantamount to surrender, but it promised a peace treaty based upon the Fourteen Points, with the two reservations excepted and another reservation confirming recognition of Czech independence.

No one knew better than Wilson what hard trials

lay ahead and how much he would need the support
of the American people to meet them. He had been
particularly alarmed by what seemed to be a surging
demand, voiced most raucously by nationalistic Republicans led by Roosevelt, for a drive to Berlin
and a harsh peace. Senator Ashurst came to the White
House on October 14 to tell Wilson that he would
be destroyed if he did not yield to the public demand. "So far as my being destroyed is concerned,"
Wilson replied, "I am willing if I can serve the country to go into a cellar and read poetry the remainder
of my life. I am thinking now only of putting the
U.S. into a position of strength and justice. I am now
playing for one-hundred years hence."

Still, he had to be prepared for the days immediately ahead. Thus he gambled in a dramatic move
to ensure Democratic success in the congressional
campaign that was reaching its climax at the very moment that he was negotiating with the Berlin government. He appealed to the country on October 25
to return a Democratic Congress. What was excep-
tional—and dangerous—was his statement that the
"return of a Republican majority to either House of
the Congress would . . . certainly be interpreted on
the other side of the water as a repudiation of my
leadership." He lost the gamble in a narrow election
on November 6, not because the voters wanted to repudiate his leadership, but, ironically, mainly because Western wheat farmers resented price ceilings
on wheat while the price of Southern cotton had been
permitted to skyrocket.

It was not a good beginning, but none the less Wilson had to proceed with preparations for the peace conference that would meet in Paris in January 1919. His first decision, which he announced on November 18, 1918, was to go to Paris as head of the American delegation. Colonel House and other friends had urged him to stay at home, on the ground that he could wield greater influence if he were not personally involved. But he believed that he alone could prevail against the forces of greed and vindicate the liberal program, and he knew that other heads of government would attend the conference. Given his deep convictions and fears, he really had no other choice.

Wilson's next decision—selection of the other peace commissioners—was perhaps more fateful if not more difficult. Tradition and expediency demanded appointment of at least one Republican and one Democratic senator. This was not possible in the circumstances. If he had chosen any senators, Wilson would have been obliged to name Senator Lodge, who would be the next chairman of the Foreign Relations Committee. Wilson thought that Lodge was utterly without scruple or character, and Lodge loathed Wilson in return. Expediency also seemed to demand appointment of someone who would represent, at least symbolically, the Republican party. Wilson simply did not trust the obvious Republican leaders, former President Taft, former Secretary of State Elihu Root, and Charles Evans Hughes. Too much, he thought, was at stake to risk division and obstruction in his own council. Thus he appointed men upon whom he thought he could rely implicitly—Colonel House, Secretary Lansing, General Tasker H. Bliss, and Henry White, a Republican career diplomat.

Wilson and his wife, the peace commissioners, and a large group of advisers and experts sailed from New York aboard the *George Washington* on December 4. Wilson was physically and emotionally exhausted, and the pleasant voyage was invigorating. He was lighthearted, almost gay as he roamed the decks, chatted with members of the crew, or entertained guests at dinner. He also had time to think about the awesome task ahead. The American delegation, he told the assembled experts on board, would be the only truly disinterested spokesmen at the conference; the Allied leaders did not even represent their own people. "Tell me what's right," he exclaimed, "and I'll fight for it." "A statement that I once made," he also told newspapermen on board, "that this should be a 'peace without victory' holds more strongly to-day than ever. The peace that we make must be one in which justice alone is the determining factor. . . . It must not be a peace of loot or spoliation. If it were such we would be an historical scourge."

The situation in Europe did not, unhappily, augur well for one who wished to fight for the right. All Europe was in shock after four years of slaughter. Britain was in the throes of a parliamentary campaign that found Prime Minister Lloyd George yielding more and more to the temptation to profit from war passions. The French were grimly determined to destroy German power forever. The Italians were clamoring for a large share of Austrian territory. Germany, still blockaded, was slowly starving and torn by class warfare. The Austro-Hungarian Empire was crumbling into ruins. And the fear of Bolshevism stalked central Europe.

Wilson and his party landed at Brest on December 13 and went straight to Paris, to be received in one of the most tumultuous demonstrations in modern history. There was more splendor than Wilson and his wife had ever seen, and there were people everywhere cheering, demonstrating, weeping. After settling in the place that was to be their first home in Paris, the residence of Prince Mûrat, just off the Place de la Concorde, the Wilsons went on a triumphal tour of England. It was wonderful to pass among the cheering crowds of London and to stay at Buckingham Palace. But for Wilson the most moving experience was a visit to his grandfather Woodrow's church at Carlisle. "It is from quiet places like this all over the world," he said in a brief speech there on December 29, "that the forces accumulate which presently will overbear any attempt to accomplish evil on a large scale. Like the rivulets gathering into the river and the river into the seas, there come from communities like this streams that fertilize the consciences of men, and it is the conscience of the world that we are trying to place upon the throne which others would usurp." Then followed a final tour through Italy, climaxed by a visit at the Quirinal Palace in Rome.

Ovations, applause, and adulation usually accorded only to messiahs of course moved Wilson profoundly, as they would any man of warm emotions. But they stirred and strengthened him without turning his head. They were, he thought, only the outward signs of the hopes of mankind everywhere for a righteous peace and an end of war, "that imperative yearning of the world," as he put it in a speech at the Guild-hall in London on December 28, "to have all dis-turbing questions quieted, to have all threats against peace silenced, to have just men everywhere come together for a common object." Was he, Woodrow Wilson, the hope of mankind, as the humble people in the throngs seemed to say? If so, he would do the best he could.

Representatives of the thirty-two nations (includ-ing the British Dominions) that had declared war against Germany gathered in the Foreign Ministry in Paris on January 18, 1919, for the plenary session opening the peace conference. There were no Ger-man delegates, as this conference had been called merely to draft a preliminary treaty that would later be hammered into final draft in negotiation with a German delegation. The threat of the collapse of central Europe and the ensuing triumph of Bolshev-ism in that area soon caused leaders at Paris to decide to press forward with all speed on a definitive treaty of peace. Detail work was assigned to some fifty-eight commissions on which small nations were well rep-resented. But important questions were first referred to a Council of Ten, composed of the heads of gov-

ernment and foreign ministers of the principal Allied and Associated Powers—the United States, Great
Britain, France, Italy, and Japan. In order to hasten
work, the unwieldy Council of Ten was superseded
on March 24, and replaced by a Council of Five,
composed of the foreign ministers of the great powers, and a Council of Four, composed of Wilson,
Lloyd George, Premier Georges Clemenceau of
France, and Premier Vittorio Orlando of Italy.

The latter group were, actually, the men who made
all ultimate decisions. Clemenceau, representative
of the sturdy, nationalistic peasants and middle classes
of France, embodied the French longing for revenge
and destruction of the power that had twice invaded
his beloved homeland during his lifetime. He was
cynical and a master of the sarcastic epigram, but he
was utterly consistent and capable of high-minded-
ness. Lloyd George embodied much that was best in
the English radical tradition. He had been the principal force behind the Liberal program that had
begun to put social and economic democracy to work
in Great Britain before 1914. He, like many other
English leaders, shared many of Wilson's objectives
for a new world based on law and justice. But he was
also mercurial in temperament, vain, ruthless, and
so much a practitioner of the doctrine of expediency
that he gave the impression of having no principles.
Orlando was a passionate orator, capable of being
moved to tears by the expression of noble ideals, and
an idealist except when Italian ambitions were involved. Then he had to yield to public clamor. All

three were tough, experienced negotiators, master politicians, determined to achieve what they and their advisers deemed to be objectives essential to their nations' security.

It was the hardest challenge in Wilson's Presidency up to this point to work constructively with such men. In the beginning, at least, he shared the prevailing American suspicion of European politics and politicians. He was, at least, a bit self-righteous about his own motives. Nor did he really understand at the outset how formidable domestic pressures limited his colleagues' freedom of action. It is remarkable that the encounter turned out as well as it did, given, among other things, Wilson's predispositions, prejudices, normal urge to dominate, and lack of experience in dealing face to face with men who were his equals in authority.

To compound these difficulties, there was the further handicap of lukewarmness in Wilson's own entourage. General Bliss and Henry White worked faithfully and accepted Wilson's decisions without complaint. But Lansing sulked throughout most of the conference (and afterward), most assuredly because he resented Wilson's domination. The greatest liability was Colonel House, upon whom Wilson depended most for expression of his own point of view. The trouble was, in part, that House took the English or French point of view over Wilson's, or he was so eager to achieve a settlement quickly that he thought it was necessary to compromise and give away. House also found it more difficult than usual to curb his egotism. He was often sure that he knew much more about peacemaking than Wilson. It did not matter so much as long as Wilson was in active command of the American delegation, but trouble was bound to occur once Wilson permitted House to speak for him. Wilson returned, for example, to the United States in February for the end of the congressional session. "House has given away everything I had won before we left Paris," Wilson told his wife after their return to Paris. "He has compromised on every side, and so I have to start all over again and this time it will be harder, as he has given the impression that my delegates are not in sympathy with me."

Wilson, on the other hand, had certain large advantages. He was in fact the only leader at Paris representing the only country with absolutely nothing selfish to ask. This gave him a commanding moral position, even if the opportunity to be altruistic was sheer good luck. He was, moreover, the hardest working major statesman at Paris and incomparably the best generally informed. Finally, he was the one man who could view the settlement as a whole, without the distorting influence of national interest.

His methods as negotiator also won respect and results. He had not come to Paris thinking that he could impose his own solutions exclusively. He had come to act as what he thought should be the conscience of mankind and, more specifically, as the voice of the American people. Here is what is right, he would say. Here is what the American people, indeed all the peoples of the western world, will approve and be willing to support in the long run. This proposal is not only wrong but also unrealistic. If you adopt it you will imperil the whole peace structure; indeed, you will endanger American ratification of the peace treaty. In controversies over mere details Wilson would seek or accept a compromise. On some matters of principle he yielded after fighting hard, when refusal to compromise would have produced worse results. On other questions of principle he was absolutely adamant. But he had only one bludgeon—the threat to leave the conference and make a separate peace. He could use this weapon only once or twice, so catastrophic would have been the consequences of carrying through.

A final advantage stemmed from Wilson's rapid progress toward a remarkable understanding of European problems. Actually, he gained a much better grasp of the European point of view than his colleagues ever gained of the American point of view. He won the respect, even the admiration, of Clemenceau and Orlando and many British leaders. The great tragedy of the encounter was the lack of sympathy and understanding between Lloyd George and Wilson. Lloyd George resented Wilson's moral claims and distrusted him instinctively as a man of principle. Wilson had an ill-disguised contempt for Lloyd George's inconsistency. Temperamental differences, among others, prevented really fruitful collaboration (but certainly not all collaboration) between the two men who should have had, actually did have, the most objectives in common.

Debate and decision on many issues proceeded without great commotion to the relatively easy reso⋅ lution of many details of the treaty with Germany, for all Allied statesmen were quick to acknowledge the binding authority of the Fourteen Points when it served national interests to do so. Thus Belgian independence was restored; Alsace-Lorraine was returned to France; Czech independence, already established in fact, was confirmed; a new Polish nation with access to the sea was created; Germany was rather thoroughly disarmed, and provisions were made to begin negotiations for general disarmament; and the Balkan states were given opportunity for free development under safeguards to protect minorities and international trade. Moreover, the settlement of colonial claims did at least provide definite international safeguards, through a mandate system under the League of Nations, to assure the progressive development of colonial peoples toward autonomy and eventual independence.

The only important controversy over a League of Nations concerned the time when it should be es⋅ tablished. Colonel House and many of the European leaders wanted to proceed as quickly as possible to completion of the treaty with Germany, and then to convoke a second conference to draft a constitution for the League. Wilson, suspecting (unfairly) that his colleagues really wanted to scuttle the project entirely, insisted that the constitution be written into the German treaty, and that the League should be the agency to oversee enforcement of that and other treaties. He had his way, though not without making concessions in return. He was also chairman of the commission appointed to draft the League's constitution, or Covenant. The French quite frankly wanted a league of victors with a powerful army— in other words, a *European* security agency which they would dominate. Wilson wanted a league of all nations, the vanquished as well as the victors, in other words a universal alliance dependent upon the organized opinion of mankind and the leadership of the great powers for its effectiveness. Wilson yielded to the French demand for *postponement* of German membership. But he had the strong support of Lord Robert Cecil of Great Britain and Jan Christian Smuts of the Union of South Africa, and he got the kind of league that he wanted, mainly by hard, patient work on many drafts of the Covenant. It was, Wilson said, when he presented the Covenant to the second plenary session of the conference on January 25, "a living thing . . . a definite guarantee of peace . . . against the things which have just come near bringing the whole structure of civilization into ruin."

This living thing was in Wilson's eyes quite obviously the hope of the future, the best guarantee of peace. The French were somewhat less than reassured and they wanted other guarantees. They wanted, most importantly, to destroy German power forever

by tearing the west bank of the Rhine from the
Reich by creating one or more so-called republics
under French influence. Wilson, with Lloyd George's
help, opposed this demand with grim and unrelenting determination all through the early weeks of the
conference, arguing that dismemberment of Germany in the west would outrageously violate the
Pre-Armistice Agreement and lead inevitably to another European war. Clemenceau had to yield on this
point, but only because Wilson and Lloyd George
agreed to sign treaties promising British and American assistance in the event that France were attacked
by Germany. Wilson, in fact, wrote out the promise
with a pencil on a scrap of paper.

The controversy over reparations was even more
prolonged and bitter. Wilson, appalled by the wan-
ton German destruction that he had seen in France
and Belgium, was as much determined as the French
to see that proper reparation was made. Thus he
consented, because he thought that it was just, to
immediate Allied seizure of some five billion dollars'
worth of German property. He also consented, under
extreme pressure, to three severe French demands:
(1) that Germany should be forced to bear the costs
of disability pensions to Allied veterans and their
families, on the fictional ground that these were
really civilian damages; (2) that Germany and her
allies should be compelled to admit (in Article 231)
entire responsibility for the war and all war losses
and damages (the following article, however, limited
this liability to civilian damages); and (3) that the

French should have the right to occupy the Rhine-
land beyond a stipulated period if the Germans failed
to meet their reparations obligations.

Compromises such as these were not achieved, however, without struggle and some personal bitterness.
One specific disagreement, for example, threatened
to disrupt the conference altogether. The Germans
while retreating had wantonly flooded and wrecked
French coal mines, and Clemenceau demanded pos-
session of the coal-rich Saar Valley in western Germany as compensation. Wilson fought hard against
the demand, saying that transfer of German territory
to France would only incubate another war. Tempers
flared, and Clemenceau accused Wilson of being pro-
German. Wilson held his tongue until the afternoon
session, but then he replied so eloquently that even
Clemenceau was momentarily moved. Soon, however,
he was hammering at Wilson on the Saar question
(and other matters as well). Wilson fell ill with in-
fluenza on April 3, and Clemenceau intensified his
pressure. It was more than Wilson could endure. "I
can never sign a Treaty made on these lines," he told
his wife, "and if all the rest of the delegates have
determined on this, I will not be a party to it. If I
have lost my fight, which I would not have done had
I been on my feet, I will retire in good order; so we
will go home." On that same day, April 7, he sent
a cablegram to Washington asking how long it would
take to put the *George Washington* in readiness for
a trip to France.

It was no bluff, and Clemenceau had to compro-

mise on the Saar issue. The French got ownership of
the Saar mines for a fifteen-year period, but German
sovereignty in the Saar Valley was only suspended,
and the area was to be governed by a League of Nations commission. Finally, the people of the Saar
Valley should have the right to vote at the end of
the fifteen-year period whether to live under French
or German sovereignty.

More important, Wilson knew, were the larger
questions of who should determine future German
reparations payments, and how the reckoning should
be made. The French, supported usually by Lloyd
George, demanded in effect a blank check: Germany
should be bled as long as possible. Wilson, with the
strong support of his financial advisers, fought hard
to secure agreement on a fixed sum for reparations
and proposed creation of a Reparations Commission
to prepare a schedule of payments for a definite period. These, Wilson knew, were the crucial safeguards,
and he fought stubbornly, countering French demands with eloquent appeals to right and reason.
He had to yield his demand for a fixed sum when
Clemenceau and Lloyd George combined against
him, but he was determined to hold the line by
limiting Germany's obligation by a time limit on
payments. Then Wilson fell ill, and Colonel House,
representing the American President in the Council
of Four on April 5, supported the French position.

There were other controversies and crises equally
bitter and almost as important as those provoked by
French demands for security and material com-

pensation. How much easier and agreeable it would have been to have yielded and accepted obfuscating language in return! It simply was not possible for Wilson to take the easy way when he thought that it was the wrong way.

There was, for example, a nagging dispute with the Japanese delegation over German rights in the Shantung Province of China. The Japanese legal position was impregnable. They had overrun the entire German concession in the Shantung Province in 1914. They had then proceeded to exact a treaty from China recognizing their rights as successors to Germany in the province and had, besides, obtained confirmation of these rights from the British, French, and Russian governments. It was precisely the kind of secret, selfish diplomacy that Wilson detested most, and he took up the Chinese cause with a nearly religious zeal, urging the Japanese to make their own contribution to the new world order by forgoing conquest. He fought alone—the Japanese were implacable, and the Allied governments were bound to support them—and he had to yield. But he did obtain verbal promises from the Japanese to restore full political sovereignty in the Shantung Province to China. The Japanese later honored this pledge.

Wilson also bore the major brunt of battle in an acrimonious dispute over Italian claims to parts of the former Austro-Hungarian Empire. Italy had entered the war in 1915 under the terms of the Treaty of London, in which the Allies had promised her the Austrian Trentino, or Tyrol, up to the

Brenner Pass; the district of Trieste; and the Dalma-
tian coast below the port of Fiume. There would
have been no conflict if the Italians had kept their
appetites within reasonable bounds. Wilson approved
Italian acquisition of the Trentino on strategic
grounds, even though it violated the principle of
self-determination, and of Trieste, which was certainly in accord with the principle of self-determination. Then the Italians demanded Fiume, which had
been promised to the Serbs by the Treaty of London
and would be the only good outlet to the sea for the
new state of Yugoslavia. Lloyd George and Clemenceau resented Italian pretensions nearly as much as
Wilson, but they let him fight the grueling battle
over Fiume almost alone. It finally exhausted Wilson's patience, and in a notable indiscretion he
appealed over the heads of Orlando and Foreign
Minister Sidney Sonnino directly to the Italian
people on April 23. Orlando and Sonnino went home
more in bluff than huff. They returned when it was
evident that Wilson would not yield.

The chaotic and changing situation in Russia and
the menace of Bolshevism in central Europe hung like
a pall over the men at Paris. Wilson had somewhat
romantic notions about the capacity of the Russian
people for democratic self-government and self-
determination at that time. He also (like other western leaders) was badly informed about events in
Russia. He perhaps failed to grasp an opportunity to
end the civil war in Russia by agreement with the
Bolsheviks that might have palliated their hostility

to the west. We will never know what might have happened if he had responded to Lenin's offer brought back from Russia in early April by the American diplomat William C. Bullitt. It proposed an armistice in the Russian civil war, amnesty on all sides, withdrawal of Allied aid to the anti-Bolsheviks, and a lifting of the Allied blockade against the Bolsheviks. The Big Four decided instead to recognize the anti-Bolshevik government of Admiral Alexander V. Kolchak. Mistakes were inevitable in the confused circumstances of the time.

In spite of it all, Wilson worked out what most experts would now agree were the *right principles* upon which to base policy. In all the discussion about Russia during the peace conference, Wilson affirmed and defended two fundamental principles—that the Russian people must be given an opportunity to solve their internal problems without outside interference, and that Bolshevism was a revolutionary response to deep-rooted wrongs and could be met only by removing its causes, not by force. He had learned his lessons well in failing to impose his own control upon the Mexican Revolution. He had also learned something about the mighty power of a movement directed against economic and social injustice. "Trying to stop a revolutionary movement by troops in the field," he warned the Council of Four, "is like using a broom to hold back a great ocean." Thus he turned a deaf ear to all suggestions (pressed most ardently by the British leader, Winston S. Churchill) for military intervention in Russia proper, and he

refused to send American troops to Vienna to help
stem what seemed to be an onrushing Bolshevik tide
after a communist coup in Hungary.

The German treaty had been completed by the
end of April, and the Foreign Minister of the new
German Republic appeared before a plenary session
on May 7, to receive a copy. A German delegation
returned to Paris on May 29 to present a comprehensive reply that pointed up forthrightly, if somewhat
truculently, the treaty's incongruities and violations
of the Pre-Armistice Agreement. It also hinted that
the German government would refuse to ratify the
document unless certain important changes were
made. Lloyd George in panic proposed to make
sweeping revisions. Wilson agreed to changes favorable to Germany in arrangements to determine the
boundary line between Germany and Poland. He
tried to win support again for his proposal of a fixed
sum for reparations, and, failing in this effort, approved when Lloyd George proposed to offer a sop to
German public opinion. But Wilson closed ranks with
Clemenceau in reaffirming other major provisions.
Either the treaty as it generally stood was just, or it
was unjust, he said. He would not agree to change it
merely to assure German ratification. He believed
that it was the best possible settlement and a just one,
on the whole. He was confident that time and American mediatory influence would heal many wounds
of war in the future. He did not fret about inevitable mistakes, most importantly, because he knew that
the treaty contained something new in the history of

peace settlements—self-correcting machinery for own revision in the League of Nations.

The German National Assembly at Weimar approved the treaty on June 23, and the formal ceremony of signing was held five days later in the great Hall of Mirrors in the Versailles Palace, where Bismarck's German Empire had been proclaimed only forty-eight years before. All Paris was festooned and delirious with excitement. Wilson drove with his wife to Versailles for the brief and almost anticlimactic ceremony. Its conclusion at 3:40 in the afternoon was signaled by booming cannon. The Wilsons returned to their residence; shortly afterward they went to a final state dinner at the Élysée Palace. Later that night they boarded a special train for Brest and the trusty *George Washington*.

Chapter Eight

BREAKING THE HEART OF
THE WORLD

The return home was another triumphal procession. Warships and throngs of people greeted the *George Washington* in New York on July 8, 1919, and there were ten thousand people in Union Station to welcome Wilson when he arrived in Washington on the same day. The outpouring of affection was genuine enough, but it was, unhappily for Wilson, also somewhat misleading. Ugly developments were cooling idealistic ardor and diverting public concern into channels unrelated to the peace settlement. Pent-up racial tensions, caused in part by a massive movement of Southern Negroes into Northern and Midwestern urban centers, were bursting into bloody race riots in Chicago, Omaha, Washington, and elsewhere. The country was in the throes of a dizzy postwar inflation and speculative mania and distraught by the worst outbreak of strikes in the nation's history. Fear of Bolshevism and radicalism, set off by a general strike in Seattle, an unsuccessful bomb plot aimed at a number of federal officials and others, and an irresponsible press, gripped the American people in the first "Red Scare."

More disquieting still to Wilson's advisers were the many signs of profound dissatisfaction with, even bitter resentment against, the Versailles Treaty. Earlier criticism, and a "round robin" resolution signed by thirty-seven senators on March 4, 1919, had prompted Wilson to obtain changes in the League Covenant permitting member nations to withdraw from the League after due notice, exempting domestic questions from the League's jurisdiction, and according recognition to the Monroe Doctrine. These changes had won few new supporters to the President's side. German-Americans protested that the Treaty was a base betrayal of the Pre-Armistice Agreement. The normally Democratic Irish-Americans were in rebellion because the peace settlement had not somehow included independence for Ireland. Pacifists and idealists were shocked and morally outraged by the seemingly harsh provisions. Their reaction had been forecast when several young liberals in the American and British delegations, including Bullitt and the English economist John Maynard Keynes, had resigned in disgust before the Paris Peace Conference ended. Most important, old ingrained isolationist attitudes and anti-European prejudices were beginning to crystallize into a formidable opposition to the very idea of American membership in the League of Nations.

These signs of domestic disunity and opposition did not seem to worry Wilson in the prelude to the debate in the Senate over ratification. He knew, to be sure, that a hard struggle impended. Republican senators would of course oppose the Treaty. But the Senate would consent to ratification in the end. Repudiation, withdrawal, and wrecking of the settlement were simply unthinkable. Moreover, the people would crush any man who dared to obstruct fulfillment of the age-old dream of peace. "I do not think hypothetical questions are concerned. *The Senate is going to ratify the treaty,*" Wilson told a reporter who had asked him if the Versailles Treaty could be ratified without important alterations.

Indeed, Wilson was in triumphant mood when he presented the Treaty formally to the Senate on July 10, 1919. After "informing" senators that a world settlement had been made, he took high ground in recommending prompt approval. The League of Nations, he exclaimed, was the hope of mankind. "Dare we reject it and break the heart of the world?" He gave the answer eloquently: "The stage is set, the destiny disclosed. It has come about by no plan of our conceiving, but by the hand of God who led us into this way. We cannot turn back. We can only go forward, with lifted eyes and freshened spirit, to follow the vision. It was of this that we dreamed at our birth. America shall in truth show the way. The light streams upon the path ahead, and nowhere else."

Alignments in the Senate clarified while Senator Lodge, chairman of the Foreign Relations Committee, held prolonged and often useless hearings on the Treaty during the next six weeks. Most of the forty-seven Democratic senators would approve ratification without amendments or reservations for party reasons and because they really approved the settlement. A group of extreme isolationists, called irreconcilables (four Democrats and six Republicans) would fight ratification, and above all American membership in the League, to the bitter end. The great majority of the forty-nine Republican senators would approve ratification, but only after insisting upon (and perhaps obtaining) amendments or reservations to preserve full American freedom of action in the League. They took their first cue from Elihu Root, who on June 21 had recommended adoption of reservations to safeguard the Monroe Doctrine, clarify the right of member nations to withdraw from the League, and free the United States from any obligations under Article X of the Covenant. This article, the cornerstone of the new collective security system, guaranteed the political independence and territorial integrity of member nations. The majority of Re-

publican senators were, therefore, strong reservationists, and their parliamentary leader was Senator
Lodge. He was an extreme nationalist, sardonically
critical of Wilson's international ideals, and he would
probably have welcomed the outright rejection of
the Treaty. But as Republican leader in the Senate
he had to defend the common ground on which most
Republicans stood. Finally, there were about twelve
Republican senators who generally approved the
Treaty as it stood and wanted nothing more than
reservations to clarify American obligations. They
were known as mild reservationists.

Wilson did what he could to rally supporters during the oppressive weeks in July and August as the
Foreign Relations Committee's hearings ground on.
He welcomed the Committee members to the White
House on August 19 and submitted cheerfully to
their searching questions for three hours. One epi-
sode in this encounter has provoked much controversy ever since. Senators William E. Borah and
Hiram Johnson of California, both irreconcilables,
asked Wilson whether he had known about the Allied
secret treaties before he went to Paris. Wilson replied
that he had not. It subsequently came out that he
almost certainly had seen a copy of the Treaty of
London and was probably informed about other
Allied understandings during the first months of
American participation in the war. It can now be
said with some certainty that Wilson had simply for-
gotten these facts when he answered Borah's and

Johnson's questions. Wilson took the additional step of inviting some twenty Republican senators, most of them being mild reservationists, to the White House for private conferences. He explained the controverted provisions of the Treaty frankly and appealed for their support on the high ground of the interests of mankind.

It was obvious to Wilson by mid-August that he was losing ground. He had not converted any strong reservationists. He had, perhaps, made some impression on the mild reservationists, but he could not rely on them. Worst of all, the irreconcilables and other enemies of the Treaty were making dangerous headway in the debate that was now proceeding furiously throughout the country. There was no choice, Wilson concluded, but to go to the people and purify the wells of public opinion that had been poisoned by demagogues and falsifiers. As it turned out, it was perhaps the most fateful decision of his career. He was physically weakened by his labors at Paris, and Dr. Grayson warned that the ardors of a long speaking tour might endanger his life. He canceled plans for a tour in early August after listening to Grayson's warning, but he decided later in the month that he had to go. "I do not want to do anything foolhardy," he told Grayson, "but the League of Nations is now in its crisis, and if it fails I hate to think what will happen to the world. You must remember that I, as Commander in Chief, was responsible for sending our soldiers to Europe. In the crucial test in the trenches they did not turn back—and I cannot turn back now. I cannot put my personal safety, my health in the balance against my duty—I must go."

Wilson, accompanied by his wife, the faithful Grayson, and a large group of White House staff members and correspondents, left Washington on their special train on September 3. They went straight to the Middle West, where isolationist sentiments were strongest. Wilson spoke everywhere in good temper and with superb clarity, carefully explaining and defending the major provisions of the Versailles Treaty. But he devoted his supreme effort to defense of the League of Nations. It was as if he thought that he could educate the American people overnight for the world leadership that he said history now demanded of them. Their isolation, he said, was over, whether they liked it or not; they would inevitably play a vital role in the affairs of the world. The only question was whether they would play that role constructively in the League of Nations, or irresponsibly by standing alone. The much condemned Article X, he said over and over, was the very foundation stone of the new system of world-wide security. As he put it at Reno:

> Article X is the heart of the enterprise. Article X is the test of the honor and courage and endurance of the world. Article X says that every member of the League . . . solemnly engages to respect and preserve as against external aggression the territorial integrity and existing political independence of the other members of the League. If you do that, you

have absolutely stopped ambitious and aggressive war. . . . As against external aggression, as against ambition, as against the desire to dominate from without, we all stand together in a common pledge, and that pledge is essential to the peace of the world.

The warm reception of Midwestern audiences changed into roaring, intoxicating applause as Wilson campaigned into the West. There he found—or rather began to highlight with increasing intensity—the overriding, urgent theme. It was that American membership and leadership in the League of Nations was utterly essential to the preservation of peace, the most vital and elemental national interest of the United States. Over and over he cried out warnings like the following:

Why, my fellow citizens, nothing brings a lump into my throat quicker on this journey I am taking than to see the thronging children that are everywhere the first, just out of childish curiosity and glee, no doubt, to crowd up to the train when it stops, because I know that if by any chance we should not win this great fight for the League of Nations it would be their death warrant. They belong to the generation which would have to fight the final war, and in that final war there would not be merely seven and a half million men slain. The very existence of civilization would be in the balance.

It was matchless oratory, and Westerners had never seen such an outpouring of approval for a public leader. Crowds surging around the presidential automobile in Tacoma nearly got out of hand. The

reception was if anything more tumultuous in southern California. But for Wilson the price of achievement came high. He began to be plagued by head-
aches in Montana, on the westward leg of the journey.
They became frequent and blinding once he reached
the West Coast. He was covered with sweat after a
speech in Cheyenne. "I have caught the imagination
of the people," he told his wife, refusing to stop.
"They are eager to hear what the League stands for;
and I should fail in my duty if I disappointed them."
He had such a splitting headache that he could hardly
see during a morning speech in Denver on September
25. Then followed an even more strenuous address
in Pueblo in the evening of the same day. Dr. Grayson found him on the verge of a complete breakdown
the next morning. There was nothing to do but can-
cel the final speeches (Wilson had already traveled
8,000 miles in twenty-two days and delivered thirty-
two major and eight minor addresses), and the train
sped to Washington, arriving on September 28.

Wilson was able to walk to his automobile in
Union Station and, indeed, seemed to improve during the next two days. Then thrombosis, caused by a
clot in an artery in the brain, struck on the morning
of October 2. It paralyzed the left side of his face
and body. His life hung in the balance during the
next two and a half weeks; on one frightful occasion
it seemed that death was inevitable. But strength began to return on about October 20, and he was sitting
up and doing a little work by the end of the month.

The Senate was at this very time nearing the end

of a long debate over the Treaty of Versailles. The Democrats, with the help of the mild reservationists, defeated a number of amendments which would have required renegotiation of the Treaty. Then Senator Lodge presented fourteen reservations on behalf of the Foreign Relations Committee on November 6. Most of them were more or less unimportant, but Reservation Two, concerning Article X, declared that the United States assumed no obligations to preserve the territorial integrity or political independence of any other country, unless Congress should specifically assume such obligation by act or joint resolution. The Democratic minority leader, Gilbert M. Hitchcock of Nebraska, countered with five reservations, four of which Wilson had substantially approved before he left on the Western tour. They simply sought to clarify the American understanding of Article X and other provisions of the Treaty.

Lodge beat down the Hitchcock reservations with the help of the irreconcilables and then won adoption of his own. The issue was finally clear after weeks of confusing maneuvering and obscuring discussion—whether to approve the Treaty virtually outright, with all that that implied, or whether to approve it with reservations that repudiated all legal and moral obligations and promised American co-operation in the League of Nations only when such co-operation was agreeable to Congress.

The decision, actually, was Wilson's, as Lodge and the great majority of Republicans had made it clear that Wilson could have ratification only on their

terms. They could also count on the irreconcilables
for help in defeating ratification with the Hitchcock
reservations. Wilson saw Hitchcock at the White
House on November 17. He was adamant against the
Lodge reservations, particularly the reservation to
Article X. It was, he said, "a nullification of the
Treaty and utterly impossible." "If the opponents
are bent on defeating this Treaty," he went on, "I
want the vote of each Republican and Democrat
recorded, because they will have to answer to the
country in the future for their acts." With Hitchcock's help the President drafted a letter instructing
Democrats in the Senate. The Lodge resolution of
ratification, he said, did not provide for ratification
"but, rather, for the nullification of the Treaty." All
true friends of the Treaty would refuse to support
the Lodge resolution. Then the door would probably be open for a genuine resolution of ratification.

The Senate went through the predetermined mo-
tions of a vote on November 19. The irreconcilables
joined the Democrats to defeat ratification with the
Lodge reservations by a vote of thirty-nine ayes to
fifty-five nays. Lodge then permitted a vote on a
resolution by Senator Oscar W. Underwood of Alabama for ratification without reservations. The irreconcilables now joined the Republicans to defeat this
resolution by a vote of thirty-eight ayes to fifty-three
nays. Only one Republican mild reservationist, Senator Porter J. McCumber of North Dakota, joined
the Democrats in supporting the resolution. The
Senate then voted to adjourn.

It was not the end, for leaders and people everywhere refused to accept the verdict, and a powerful pressure mounted in December 1919 and January 1920 for some compromise. Prominent Republicans who had taken leadership in a nonpartisan movement for the League—including former President Taft and Herbert Hoover—scores of editors, and representatives of organizations with memberships numbering from twenty to thirty million Americans called for action. Colonel House, now no longer welcome at the White House, urged his old friend to capitulate. William J. Bryan was in the field campaigning for ratification with the Lodge reservations, if this were necessary to obtain the Senate's approval.

The demand seemed overwhelming, and a bipartisan conference of senators met in Washington during the last two weeks of January 1920 to find common ground. Even Lodge weakened and joined the conferees, and for a moment it seemed that he might approve a reservation on Article X that Democrats could support. Then the Republican irreconcilables threatened to bolt the party and organize an independent anti-League movement if there were any yielding on the second reservation. Lodge promptly withdrew from the bipartisan conference and refused ever afterward to make even a show of concession. It was probably what he wanted to do anyway.

Wilson had meanwhile been gaining strength and laying plans of his own for a new campaign. By mid-December he was again *au courant* with affairs of state. He listened courteously when friends, even his wife, urged him to meet Lodge halfway. But he did not believe that compromise was necessary. He had a deep and abiding faith in the good sense of the American people and their ability to make right decisions when they knew all the facts. He knew the massive power of public opinion in a democracy. He had seen it force a reluctant Senate to consent to tariff and banking reform years before. The people had never failed to respond in crises in the past. They would respond now and smite the obstructionists in the Senate. It was his job to get well so that he could take to the field again.

Wilson had been considering strategy in the event of the defeat of a ratification resolution even before the first Senate vote on the Treaty. "I am a sick man," he told Hitchcock on November 17, ". . . but I am going to debate this issue with these gentlemen in their respective states whenever they come up for re-election if I have breath enough in my body to carry on the fight. . . . And I will get their political scalps when the truth is known to the people." In the aftermath of the first Senate vote he still believed that victory was certain if only the people could decide.

But how could the people be given an opportunity to make the choice? Wilson found, or thought that he had found, a breath-taking answer. He would challenge the fifty-seven senators opposed to ratification without strong reservations (or to ratification at all) to resign and go to the people for immediate re-election in special elections on the basis of their records. If a majority of them were re-elected, Wilson and the Vice-President would resign, so that a Republican appointed previously as Secretary of State could assume the Presidency. Wilson prepared this plan in mid-December, but discussions with the Attorney General soon persuaded him that it was neither constitutionally nor technically feasible.

A new plan slowly began to take shape in Wilson's mind during late December and early January. If the Senate obstructionists would not yield, he would run for a third term and take the fight to the people. If he won he would obtain ratification of the Treaty and then resign. As a first step—and also in order to thwart Bryan's campaign to commit the Democratic party to ratification even with the Lodge reservations—Wilson drafted a letter to be read to Democrats at their annual Jackson Day dinner on January 8. He was certain, he said, that the overwhelming majority of the people desired ratification of the Treaty without crippling reservations. But if there was any doubt as to what the people thought on the question, "the clear and single way out is to submit it for determination at the next election to the voters of the Nation, to give the next election the form of a great and solemn referendum."

All of Wilson's plans were of course tentative, to be put into execution only if the Senate refused again to give its consent to ratification without crippling reservations. Actually, he did not believe that Lodge and his colleagues would, could refuse to surrender in the final showdown. Meanwhile, he could only

wait patiently, maintain control of his forces in the
Senate, and do what he could to strengthen the public movement for ratification. He was gaining
strength all the time. He decided early in February
to clean his own house by dismissing Lansing. The
Secretary of State had earlier confided his contempt
for the League to William C. Bullitt, and Bullitt had
repeated Lansing's remarks to the Foreign Relations
Committee. Wilson requested Lansing's resignation
on February 7, using as a pretext the fact that
Lansing had called Cabinet meetings on his own authority. He then appointed Bainbridge Colby, a New
York lawyer, to Lansing's place. A few days later Wilson addressed a stinging note to the Allied leaders
accusing them of disloyalty in preparing a settlement
of the Fiume controversy awarding the disputed city
to Italy, and threatening to withdraw the Treaty
from the Senate if they proceeded on their own.

The Senate meanwhile had resumed discussion of
the Treaty in an atmosphere of new optimism en-
gendered by signs that Democrats would come to
agreement with Lodge on his own terms. Wilson was
appalled and shocked. He refused to see individual
senators who wanted to talk of compromise. Then,
on March 8, he addressed a letter to Hitchcock to be
shown to Democrats in the upper house. Article X,
Wilson said, was a moral obligation, a pledge of good
faith. Either the United States should enter the
League with its head high, accepting responsibilities
fearlessly, or else it should retire as gracefully as possible from the concert of world powers. Every so-called

reservation, he went on, was a rather sweeping nullification of the Treaty. He had heard of "reservationists" and "mild reservationists," but he could not see the difference between a "nullifier" and a "mild nullifier."

As events soon revealed, Wilson's letter sealed the doom of the Treaty in the Senate. The Republicans were now as firmly committed to the Lodge reservations as the irreconcilables were committed to defeat of the Treaty. The only hope for winning the Senate's consent to ratification lay in the chance that enough Democrats would break away from Wilson's halter to obtain the necessary two-thirds vote for approval with the Lodge reservations. Wilson's letter of March 8 prevented this from occurring when the Senate voted for a second time on March 19, 1920. Twenty-one Democrats joined Lodge and the majority of Republicans to amass a simple majority of forty-nine to thirty-five in favor of ratification with strong reservations. But they were not enough. Twenty-three Democrats combined with the irreconcilables to defeat the Treaty; a change of seven Democratic votes would have put the Treaty across in the Senate. Wilson, of course, might well have refused to ratify the Treaty in this event.

News of the Senate's vote was telephoned at once to the White House. "I feel like going to bed and staying there," Wilson said. He could not sleep that night, and he turned to Dr. Grayson at about three in the morning and said, "Doctor, the Devil is a busy man." Later in the morning he had Grayson read

Saint Paul's consoling words from Second Corin-
thians: "We are troubled on every side, yet not
distressed; we are perplexed, but not in despair;
persecuted, but not forsaken; cast down, but not destroyed." Turning to Grayson, he said, "Doctor, if I
were not a Christian, I think I should go mad, but my
faith in God holds me to the belief that He is in some
way working out His own plans through human per-
versities and mistakes."

There was still work to do, even for one perplexed
and cast down. It was obvious that the public, confused by opponents of the League and distracted by
events at home, was rapidly losing interest in the
Treaty. It seems likely, in fact, that most thoughtful
Americans by the spring of 1920 would have preferred
an end of the matter on Lodge's terms and were beginning to regard *Wilson* as the chief obstacle to ratification. The biggest single danger in Wilson's eyes was
Bryan. He was now campaigning to prevent the Democratic national convention from making the League
a leading issue in the coming presidential campaign.

Wilson's answer to these challenges was, as usual,
bold. He was still weak and could work for only short
periods at his desk (he did not hold his first Cabinet
meeting after his illness until April 14), but the fire
of audacity burned as brightly as ever within him.
First, he rallied his party with messages to Democratic state conventions saying that Democrats were
honor-bound to make the presidential election a great
and solemn referendum on the League. Next, on
May 27, he vetoed a congressional resolution ending

the war with Germany, this, in scathing words that accused Republicans of "ineffable stain upon the gallantry and honor of the United States." Finally, he conferred with Democratic leaders during late May and early June to assure adoption of a strong League plank and make possible his own renomination. He would carry the issue to the people in one final great battle, and with God's help he would win!

It was easy enough for Wilson to have his way on the platform when the Democratic national convention met in San Francisco on June 28, even though Bryan appealed to the convention over Wilson's head. "We advocate the immediate ratification of the Treaty without reservations which would impair its essential integrity," the platform read, "but [and this clause was added in spite of Wilson's misgivings] do not oppose the acceptance of any reservations making clearer or more specific the obligations of the United States to the League associates." It was, Wilson said, a "declaration of conquering purpose which nothing could defeat."

It was not so easy to obtain the third-term nomination upon which Wilson had apparently set his heart. Democrats had gone through a preconvention campaign the outcome of which was confused by uncertainty about Wilson's purposes and plans. Attorney General A. Mitchell Palmer, who had been leading a crusade against radicals, and former Secretary of the Treasury McAdoo had emerged as the strongest candidates. McAdoo might well have won the nomination had Wilson supported him. But Wilson, as we

have seen, had another plan. It was to arrange for his
nomination by acclamation after the convention had
become deadlocked between Palmer and McAdoo.
Events went at first as Wilson had hoped, but Secretary Colby met indignant opposition when he tried
to rally Wilson's friends on July 2 and 3 for a try for
the nomination. They knew far better than Wilson
that a third-term nomination would be his death
warrant, and they refused to co-operate. There was
nothing Wilson could do but acquiesce, and the nomination went after forty-four weary ballots to a rela-
tive dark horse, Governor James M. Cox of Ohio. For
the Vice-Presidency the Democrats nominated a
young Wilsonian from New York, Franklin D. Roosevelt.

One of the saddest dramas in American history
now began to be played out upon the national stage.
Cox and Roosevelt, somewhat diffident champions of
the League, visited the White House on July 18 and
came away determined to hold high the Wilsonian
torch. No one, Cox told Wilson's secretary, could talk
to the President about the League without becoming
"a crusader in its behalf." Cox was as faithful to the
trust as the exigencies of the campaign would permit,
but his voice was not the voice of Woodrow Wilson,
and he failed utterly either to rouse the people or to
make the League the supreme issue of the campaign.
Wilson watched from the side lines sadly, never really
warming to Cox. He made one speech, to a delegation of fifteen pro-League Republicans at the White
House on October 27; and he issued only one public

appeal, on October 3, calling for a genuine national referendum on the League.

It probably mattered little what Wilson or Cox or any other Democrat did or said in the circumstances prevailing during the campaign of 1920. The country was still massively Republican. Only some unusual conjunction of events, such as had occurred in 1912 and 1916, would have made it possible for any Democrat to win. There was no unusual conjunction, and voters resumed normal voting habits. Moreover, the Republican candidate, Senator Warren G. Harding of Ohio, was sufficiently nondescript and obscure in language to appeal to all disaffected groups. He cut much ground from under Cox by saying that he favored a purified League, which he called an Association of Nations. Not until near the end of the campaign did Harding avow his intention to repudiate the League altogether. Then it was too late for a clear-cut debate, if that would ever have been possible with Harding one of the participants. The hardest blow at Democratic fortunes fell on October 14, when thirty-one of the most distinguished leaders of the Republican party, including Taft, Root, Hoover, Hughes, and Henry L. Stimson, issued a statement promising that their party would take the United States into the League and saying that Harding's election was the best assurance of American membership.

The only question after the appeal of the so-called Thirty-one was the size of Harding's majority. It must have surprised the Republican campaign managers.

Harding won 16,152,200 popular and 404 electoral votes on November 2, even breaking into the solid South by carrying Tennessee. Cox, with only 9,147,-000 popular and 127 electoral votes, was the most badly beaten Democratic candidate since Stephen A. Douglas.

Only Wilson among informed observers had failed to read the signs correctly. "You need not worry," he told the Cabinet on election day. "The American people will not turn Cox down and elect Harding. A great moral issue is involved. The people can and will see it." But he was not downcast. The faith as well as the fire was as strong as ever. The people, he told his brother-in-law soon after the election, had only been misled in a period of great trial. They would eventually find the truth and act upon it.

For Wilson there now remained only the tasks of presiding over the government until his successor could be inaugurated. They were not unhappy final months in the White House. Friends and counselors deluged him with kindnesses. His health was good enough to permit moderate work and recreation. One bright event in December was the award of the Nobel Peace Prize for 1920. On March 4, 1921, he rode with Harding to the Capitol, signed a number of bills in the President's room, and received a congressional delegation headed by Senator Lodge. They had come, Lodge said, to say that Congress had finished its business. Tautly, frigidly, Wilson replied: "I have no further communication. I would be glad if you would inform both houses and thank them for their courtesy. Good morning, sir." Then he went with Mrs.

Wilson to a new home at 2340 S Street, Northwest, in Washington. He and a group of friends had bought it as a present for Mrs. Wilson some weeks before.

The routine of life was simple, almost serene, in the house on S Street. Edith Bolling Wilson had been a constant companion since their marriage in 1915. Now she was a ministering angel whose tender care and bright love eased pain and filled long days with gladness. Living out the life of a semi-invalid consisted mainly of doing small things—going to the theater, taking drives through the Virginia hills, or seeing old friends who came on pilgrimages. Only once did Wilson attend a public function to the end —the burial of the Unknown Soldier at Arlington Cemetery on Armistice Day, 1921.

For Wilson the hardest burden was the incapacity that stemmed from physical weakness. He formed a law partnership with Bainbridge Colby soon after retirement, but he was never able to practice, and the partnership was dissolved. Wilson wanted most of all to resume work on his long-delayed magnum opus, "The Philosophy of Politics." The best that he could do by way of writing was a brief article, "The Road Away from Revolution," published in August 1923. It was a warning to Americans that their society could not survive materially unless it was redeemed by being permeated with the spirit of Christ. This meant, specifically, he said, a social and economic order based on "sympathy and helpfulness and a willingness to forego self-interest in order to promote the welfare, happiness, and contentment of others and of the community as a whole." He could have spoken and written on public affairs, but he imposed a rule of silence, saying that he meant to teach ex-Presidents how to behave. Only twice during these later years did he speak out—in an Armistice Day address delivered over radio on November 10, 1923, and in a brief speech to a crowd that came to greet him on the following day. The body was weak, but the spirit was strong. "I am not one of those who have the least anxiety about the triumph of the principles I have stood for," he told his visitors. "I have seen fools resist Providence before, and I have seen their destruction, as will come upon these again, utter destruction and contempt. That we shall prevail is as sure as that God reigns."

His physical condition improved slowly until the summer of 1923. Then in the autumn of that year the disease that had caused his stroke, arteriosclerosis, renewed its ravages. Life ebbed rapidly, even though Wilson clung to it tenaciously, and as late as January 1924 he still thought of the possibility of running for the Presidency in that year. A sudden turn for the worse occurred on January 31. Bulletins announced the fatal news, and men and women gathered in S Street to keep vigil and pray. "The machinery is worn out," Wilson said to Dr. Grayson. "I am ready." Life expired at 11:15 on Sunday morning, February 3, 1924. There were private services at the house, and the body was interred in the crypt of the Washington Cathedral.

With his passing, a new star swam into the firmament of history.

ADDITIONAL READING

I. *The Writings of Woodrow Wilson.*

Laura S. Turnbull, *Woodrow Wilson, A Selected Bibliography* (Princeton, N. J., 1948), is a good guide to Wilson's published writings and speeches.

The following works by Wilson are still available at bookstores: *Congressional Government* (Meridian Paperbacks, 1956); *The New Freedom* (Prentice-Hall Paperbacks, 1961); *Constitutional Government in the United States* (Columbia University Press, 1961); and *Leaders of Men* (T. H. Vail Motter, ed., Princeton University Press, 1952.)

Most good libraries have Wilson's other major works: *The State* (Boston, 1889, 1898, 1910, 1918); *Division and Reunion, 1829–1889* (New York, 1893, 1924); *An Old Master and Other Political Essays* (New York, 1893); *Mere Literature and Other Essays* (Boston, 1896, 1924);

George Washington (New York, 1897, 1924); *A History of the American People* (5 vols., New York, 1902, 1910, 1918). Ray S. Baker and William E. Dodd (eds.), *The Public Papers of Woodrow Wilson* (6 vols., New York, 1925–27), prints many of Wilson's incidental papers and important speeches. An important supplement is John Wells Davidson, *A Crossroads of Freedom, The 1912 Campaign Speeches of Woodrow Wilson* (New Haven, Conn., 1956).

II. *Biographies.*

Ray S. Baker, *Woodrow Wilson: Life and Letters* (8 vols., Garden City, N. Y., 1927–39) and *Woodrow Wilson and World Settlement* (3 vols., Garden City, N. Y., 1922), constitute the authorized biography and print many of Wilson's letters.

A more definitive edition of Wilson's letters, public papers, and speeches is now in preparation under the sponsorship of the Woodrow Wilson Foundation and Princeton University. It will be published, in forty-odd volumes under the title *The Papers of Woodrow Wilson,* by the Princeton University Press.

Arthur S. Link has a new multivolume biography in preparation. He has published *Wilson: The Road to the White House* (Princeton, N. J., 1947), *Wilson: The New Freedom* (Princeton, N. J., 1956), and *Wilson: The Struggle for Neutrality* (Princeton, N. J., 1960).

Arthur Walworth, *Woodrow Wilson* (2 vols., New York, 1958), is good for personal details.

The following are useful shorter biographies and biographical studies: James Kerney, *The Political Education of Woodrow Wilson* (New York, 1926); David Lawrence, *The True Story of Woodrow Wilson* (New York, 1924); Herbert C. F. Bell, *Woodrow Wilson and the People* (Garden City, N. Y., 1945); John A. Garraty, *Woodrow Wilson* (New York, 1956); and John M. Blum,

Woodrow Wilson and the Politics of Morality (New York, 1956).

Especially valuable to the reader who wants to go beyond this point are memoirs by Wilson's contemporaries: Edith Bolling Wilson, *My Memoir* (Indianapolis, 1938); Cary T. Grayson, *Woodrow Wilson: An Intimate Memoir* (New York, 1960); Josephus Daniels, *The Wilson Era* (2 vols., Chapel Hill, N. C., 1944–46); and Bernard M. Baruch, *Baruch: The Public Years* (New York, 1960). Charles Seymour (ed.), *The Intimate Papers of Colonel House* (4 vols., Boston, 1926–28), is supremely important for the entire Wilson period.

III. *Historical Monographs.*

The only general works on the period 1910–21 are Arthur S. Link, *Woodrow Wilson and the Progressive Era* (New York, 1954 and 1963); and Frederick L. Paxson, *American Democracy and the World War* (3 vols., Boston and Berkeley, Calif., 1936–48).

The following are some of the more significant specialized studies: John M. Blum, *Joe Tumulty and the Wilson Era* (Boston, 1951); Arthur S. Link, *Wilson the Diplomatist* (Baltimore, 1957); Ernest R. May, *The World War and American Isolation* (Cambridge, Mass., 1959); Charles Seymour, *American Diplomacy during the World War* (Baltimore, 1934); Laurence W. Martin, *Peace Without Victory: Woodrow Wilson and the British Liberals* (New Haven, Conn., 1958); Arno J. Mayer, *The Political Origins of the New Diplomacy, 1917–1918* (New Haven, Conn., 1959); Victor S. Mamatey, *The United States and East Central Europe; 1914–1918* (Princeton, N. J., 1957); George F. Kennan, *Russia Leaves the War* (Princeton, N. J., 1956), and *The Decision to Intervene* (Princeton, N. J., 1958); Thomas A. Bailey, *Woodrow Wilson and the Lost Peace* (New York, 1944), and *Woodrow Wilson and the Great Be-*

trayal (New York, 1945); Herbert Hoover, *The Ordeal of Woodrow Wilson* (New York, 1958); Seth P. Tillman, *Anglo-American Relations at the Paris Peace Conference of 1919* (Princeton, N. J., 1961); and Wesley M. Bagby, *The Road to Normalcy, The Presidential Campaign and Election of 1920* (Baltimore, 1962).

INDEX

185

ABOUT THE AUTHOR

ARTHUR S. LINK was born in New Market, Virginia, on August 8, 1920, and was educated in the public schools of North Carolina. He received the bachelor's degree with highest honors from the University of North Carolina in 1941 and the Ph.D. degree from the same institution in 1945, after an additional year of graduate work at Columbia University. He has taught American history at North Carolina State College, the University of North Carolina, Northwestern University, and Princeton University, where he has been Professor of History and Director of the Woodrow Wilson Papers since 1960. He has been, since 1958, Editor-in-Chief of *The Papers of Woodrow Wilson*, sponsored jointly by the Woodrow Wilson Foundation and Princeton University.

Dr. Link has held Rosenwald, Rockefeller, and Guggenheim fellowships and has twice been a member of the Institute for Advanced Study in Princeton. He was the Albert Shaw Lecturer at the Johns Hopkins University in 1956 and the Harmsworth Professor of American History at Oxford University in 1958–59. He was awarded the degree of Litt.D. by Bucknell University in 1961 and the University of North Carolina in 1962, and the L.H.D. by Washington College in 1962. He is the author of nine other books, six of them on Woodrow Wilson and his time, and was awarded the Bancroft Prize for *Wilson: The New Freedom*, in 1957, and *Wilson: The Struggle for Neutrality*, in 1961.

He married Margaret Douglas in 1945 and they have four children. Dr. Link, a Presbyterian elder, is active in the work of the United Presbyterian Church as a member of various boards and committees.